Bitcoin and Cryptocurrency 2021

The Ultimate Crypto Trading and Investing Guide to Profit During the 2021 Bull Run and Change Your Life!

Bitcoin Trading

Learn the Secret Technical Analysis Strategies to Make Money during the 2021 Cryptocurrency Bull Run and Build Real Wealth - Day Trading Tips for Beginners!

By

Charles Swing

&

Masaru Nakamoto

Additionally, the information in the following pages is intended only for informational purposes and should thus be thought of as universal. As befitting its nature, it is presented without assurance regarding its prolonged validity or interim quality. Trademarks that are mentioned are done without written consent and can in no way be considered an endorsement from the trademark holder.

Table of Contents

Introduction

Bitcoin has taken the world by storm once again when it crossed $20,000 per BTC in December of last year.

A lot of people are trying to improvise themselves as professional traders and are losing a lot of money, only helping those who actually know what they are doing accumulate an incredible amount of wealth.

To join the club of the few traders that actually make it, you need the right strategies and the right mindset. Notice how we did not include a large initial capital. In fact, while having more money to trade with means having more fire power, it is not necessary to have thousands of dollars to be profitable and build wealth.

In fact, when we started trading cryptocurrencies we only had a few hundreds to put into the market, but that sum yielded us thousands and thousands of dollars.

In this book you are going to discover all the strategies that have allowed us to take our trading skills to the next level. If you apply them diligently we are sure you are going to see amazing results in a relative short period of time.

Please, stay away from all the shiny objects of the cryptocurrency world. Just choose one cryptocurrency pair, study it deeply and then milk it like a cash cow!

To your success!

Charles Swing and *Masaru Nakamoto*

Chapter 1 - An Introduction to Trading Indicators

The discipline of technical analysis consists of tools, called technical indicators which, usually based on statistical calculations and models, are used in order to interpret the performance of cryptocurrencies.

Technical analysis indicators

Within the family of technical indicators there are specific categories of instruments, each of which is best suited to the specific reference market. Among these, a fundamental division is given by leading indicators and lagging indicators. While the first of the two terms means a means of statistical forecasting of the future trend of prices (based on the detection and study of previous prices), the second focuses its attention on the signal given by the market trend.

Some indicators in the leading category are the Stochastic Oscillator and RSI (Relative Strength Indicator). Instead, indicators that belong to the lagging group are simple and exponential moving averages, MACD, Supertrend, ADX. and Parabolic Sar.

Differences between indicators and oscillators

In this regard it is also necessary to make a clarification, namely that inherent in the difference between the more common term of indicator and that of oscillator. The term indicator refers to an instrument that does not have a predefined range of movement and that instead tends to float across balance lines.

On the contrary, the oscillator is an instrument that assumes values included within a defined range, the calculation of which presupposes a normalization which in turn ends in determining the maximum and minimum levels that can be reached. This binds the oscillator to stay within a predetermined range of values, where the maximum and minimum thresholds usually coincide with overbought and oversold areas (and therefore, to sell and buy signals).

The tools of technical analysis

To move within the technical analysis it is necessary to know accurately the tools that operate in it and the differences between them in terms of characteristics and effectiveness with respect to market applicability. The use of indicators, in fact, can be an object of confusion if used incorrectly or if placed in the wrong context. The main errors may be the overinterpretation of the market, the false signal of a trend and, above all, the incongruity given by an excess of indicators applied to the same coin.

Similarly, when a signal from one indicator is confirmed by the signal from another indicator of a different category or from an oscillator, it will be more reliable and precise.

Types of indicators (and oscillators)

Among the main indicators of technical analysis on the market, it is possible to identify the following four different categories.

- Trend indicators;
- Indicators in Absence of Trend;
- Volume indicators;
- Volatility Indicators.

There is also a fifth category, which goes by the name of Cycle Indicators. The latter, unlike the other indicators, follows a separate discipline and is the subject of study for a particular school of thought in trading called cyclical trading.

By believing that the market moves according to a pattern repeated over time, the cyclical analysis aims to exploit the "predictability" of a market that follows recurring movements. Therefore, the cycle indicators start from the idea that the prices are dominated by repeated movements over time and readable in the form of a pattern.

On this assumption, various market theories have been developed, aimed at finding which force regulates a certain pattern that is repeated in succession. Of these theories, the most famous one is the theory of Elliott Waves, named after its creator.

Four types of indicators by category

Trend indicators, as the name suggests, help in identifying a trend and helping the trader in the search for the dominant trend. This section is composed of technical instruments such as the Parabolic SAR indicator, the MACD and any type of Moving Average. Alongside these, there are various tools, also aimed at interpreting the movement in progress, such as ADL, ADX and DMI.

Indicators in the Absence of Trend, also known as oscillators, consists of tools used to evaluate the occurrence of overbought or oversold situations. The latter, used in conjunction with indicators of different origins, can help to understand when and if a new trend is underway. This type of technical tools includes the RSI (Relative Strength Indicator), the stochastic oscillator and the CCI (Commodity Channel Index).

These indicators are often generally defined as Momentum Indicators, although this definition is not appropriate to the specific use. It is in fact possible that an indicator applied to a higher time frame does not give specific indications (and highlights a lateral trend), while the same applied to the same price in a shorter time frame is significant of an ongoing trend.

The third type is represented by the Volume Indicators which, as suggested by the name itself, are used to understand the dynamics of prices through the study of volumes. These, considered in terms of trades recorded in a given period of time, look at the relationship between the volume traded and the price movement recorded. A variation supported by a consistent volume has greater validity in terms of the signal it gives. This type of technical instruments includes indicators such as Money Flow Index, OBV, Force Index, Chaikin Money Flow, and Ease of Movement.

The fourth category of indicators is the one called Volatility Indicators, which often find application not so much in explaining the dynamics of the current trend, but rather in defining two margins, one higher and one lower, within which the price makes sense. These instruments, also called range indicators, are considered fundamental in order to be able to anticipate a possible increase in volatility that can send the signal of convenience for an immediate entry or exit. Among the most common volatility indicators are the Bollinger Bands and the ATR (Average True Range).

In the next few chapters we are going to talk about specific indicators.

Chapter 2 - Moving Averages

The ease of construction and extreme simplicity of use make moving averages one of the first and most elementary chart analysis tools used by beginner traders. The application of moving averages to the price of financial instruments allows the trader a whole series of considerations. This is true from the point of view of analysis, to understand at a glance and immediately what is the current trend, but it is also true from an operational point of view, as moving averages allow us to obtain a real setup for entering the position.

Moving averages are an indispensable tool for eliminating the so-called market noise, and returning to the trader a view purified from the fluctuating trend, made up of sub-trends and small corrections, which risks distracting attention from the real direction of the analyzed market.

A moving average, as the word itself says, is calculated on a certain amount of price data (time domain) and is "mobile" because it moves from day to day precisely because of its calculation method. In practice, given an average of a certain time domain, the most recent data is added each time by eliminating the last data of the series from the calculation. So, purely as an example, if you want to calculate a 20-day moving average of prices, to update it it will be enough to add today's closing data to the series and delete the closing price of 20 days ago.

From the foregoing, some consequences are immediately evident that must be taken into consideration. In fact, the longer the domain of the moving average, the more time must pass in order to start displaying the average, and the less the average itself will be reactive to price movements.

In practical terms, a 20-day moving average represents the average value of the last 20 trading sessions with punctual data and each data will weigh for 1/20 of the series. The data that we will gradually add will affect the moving average to a lesser extent the longer the time domain under consideration. Thus, a 20-day average will be less affected by the new data than a 5-day average.

Obviously, all the chart platforms currently on the market allow you to easily represent the moving averages of prices, so that to visualize them on a graph you no longer have to worry about arming yourself with graph paper, pencil and calculator, as the pioneers of chart analysis did. We recommend you use Tradingview as your go to charting software. It’s free version is more than enough for new traders to start using indicators.

From the foregoing we understand the importance of a correct choice of the time domain which, as we have said, is inversely related to the reactivity of the average. In fact, the greater the chosen time domain, the less reactive the moving average will be.

The simplicity of construction and, nevertheless, the possibility of obtaining operational signals from the intersection between prices and their average, or - as we will immediately see - directly between two averages of different time domains, have made moving averages the chart tool most used by analysts.

In principle, we can assume that we are in the presence of an uptrend, whenever prices are above the moving average taken into consideration. The reverse is true for a bearish trend.

In the picture below we can see that the price of Bitcoin, on March 17th 2021 is above the 50 day and the 200 day moving average. It is an indication that the price is bullish.

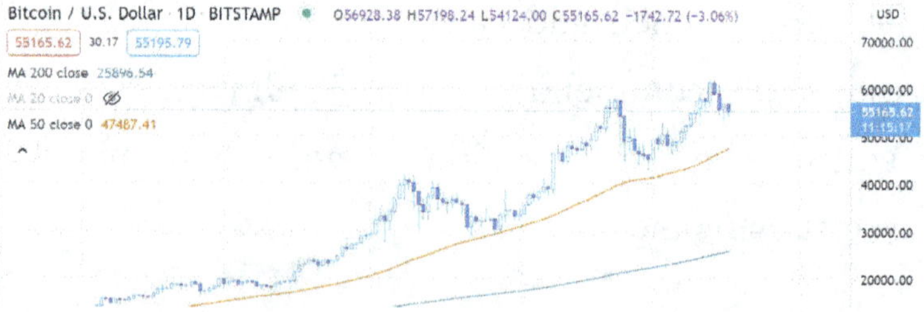

From this it follows that we can obtain a first trading signal when prices cut their moving average. If the price crosses the moving average upwards it is a long signal. On the contrary, if the cross happens in the other direction, we have a short signal.

It must be said immediately that this is not a foolproof tool. In fact, it is known that moving averages work very well in a trending market rather than in lateral movements, during which, unfortunately, false signals are frequent.

A strategy that we recommend you use when starting trading is to use the 50 day moving average as a long or short signal. When the price crosses above the 50 day moving average, you can open a long position. When the price crosses below the moving average, you can go short. Of course, never forget to set a stop loss and apply a good risk management as described in the previous chapters.

In the cryptocurrency markets, the best values of the moving averages on a daily time frame are 20, 50, 100 and 200.

Chapter 3 - Exponential Moving Averages (EMA)

This is a more refined tool than simple moving averages. Its use is a direct consequence of some shortcomings that afflict the SMA (Simple Moving Average). In fact, according to some experts, the simple moving average leads to an excessive simplification, which could prove to be very insidious in certain situations. Furthermore, the simple moving average shows a deleterious inability to give rise to a sufficiently rapid reaction in the face of sudden movements that sometimes occur on the markets.

The characteristics of the EMA indicator

Exponential moving averages are a chart tool tending to favor the most recent price action. In this respect, they actually represent a much more reliable indicator than the simple moving average. The main difference with the MVA indicator consists in the fact that each previous survey in the range of data enters the calculation, pushing the oldest data to fade their weight over time, without ever disappearing completely.

The most used exponential moving averages are those at 12 and 26 days. In these cases, the graph formulated can have as terms of reference a short-term average, just the 12-day one, and a longer-term one, for example the 60 days EMA. In the event that the short-term average crosses with the long-term one in a bullish phase, the signal that will be formed must be interpreted as a future positive trend. If the average intersects with the signal in a bearish phase, the indication to be taken will be exactly the opposite.

In the picture below you can look at the 12 and 26 days EMA for Bitcoin on March 17th, 2021.

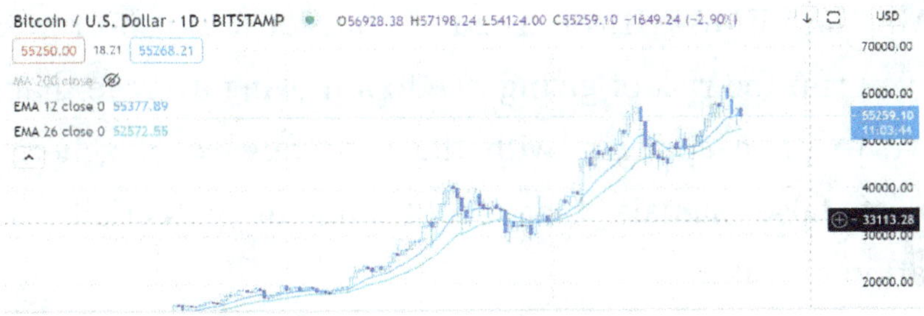

As you can see, EMAs follow the price much more closely than SMAs.

How the exponential moving average is calculated

Calculating exponential moving averages is fairly easy. In fact, it is necessary to calculate a percentage of the present value of prices and then combine the result obtained with that which resulted from the calculation of the inverse percentage of the last value taken as a reference. In practice, if we decide to give the current price value a weight of 40%, the weight to be calculated on the last reference price will consequently amount to 60%. The weight percentage is expressed by a very precise mathematical formula:

$$2 / (period + 1)$$

Precisely on the basis of this formula, if we decide to consider a period of 15 days, the weight of the percentage would be 2 / (15 + 1).

In order to be able to implement a strategy capable of proving to be successful, we must be careful to choose the most appropriate period on which to graft the calculation of the average. This is true for SMAs and EMAs. If you decide to opt for a too short period of time, you run the risk of giving rise to a moving average that is too reactive to price changes, with the consequence of generating a series of false signals that could end in potentially serious evaluation mistakes.

SMAs or EMAs?

Why should a trader use one of the two averages instead of the other? And in particular, why should a trader use the exponential moving average? Like the simple moving average, the EMA can be considered a sort of useful compass to better orientate through the pitfalls of the markets. Precisely in this sense, all traders should use them and integrate them into their strategy. Especially if you intend to operate in a short time frame where, using the exponential moving average can be particularly advantageous precisely because it is much more able to adapt to recent price changes than SMAs.

However, please keep in mind that in reality the differences are not so marked and we could conclude by stating that for all those who need to determine the primary trend it would be advisable to use the simple moving average, while the use of the exponential one can avoid the onset of false signals if trading is based on tight enough time frames.

Chapter 4 - Relative Strength Index (RSI)

Let's first look at the operating principles of the Relative Strength Index created by J. Welles Wilder who published it in his book "New Concepts in Technical Trading System" dating back to 1978.

The RSI is an instrument that measures the momentum of prices. The momentum is the speed (intensity) with which the price variation is produced. Its calculation is essentially based on the ratio between the average of the difference between the closing prices of the upward sessions with the sum of the same average and the average of the absolute value of the closing downward differences in the period considered.

Beyond the calculation criterion, which is of little interest to its user except to know the principles on which the oscillator being used is built, it appears as a line that oscillates between zero and 100.

According to the classic setting, the overbought zone is considered the threshold over 70 and the oversold zone the threshold below the value 30. The default parameter used is 14 periods. On Tradingview it can be lowered or raised to decrease or increase the sensitivity of the oscillator.

How to use the RSI

The RSI can be used to identify different operational signals. One of the classic ways is to search for divergences between prices and oscillators, as we see in the following picture.

After a sharp decline, the DOT/USD chart (DOT is the ticker symbol for Polkadot, a cryptocurrency you should definitely check out) generates two descending lows while the RSI oscillator generates two rising lows. In this case we are in the presence of a bullish divergence. The divergence manages to capture a reversal of the trend and the prices begin to rise.

Identifying divergences on this oscillator is not difficult and often these divergences give rise to important reversals, as we see in the following picture.

As we can see from the graph (CRO/USD, CRO is the ticker symbol for Crypto.com), prices make two successive increasing highs, while the oscillator generates two decreasing highs. In this case we are in the presence of bearish divergence. And the trend does not take long to make a rather important reversal.

RSI Filters

It is advisable to combine some additional filters with this indicator. In fact, such as candlestick patterns, many false signals can be generated in very strong trends. With a candlestick pattern we are able to significantly limit the stop loss, thanks to the techniques explained in the section on Japanese candlesticks.

As already mentioned at the beginning of this chapter, the RSI indicator provides us indications of relative price strength. Consequently it is not only an indicator that can provide buy and sell signals, but also has the ability to tell us which is the main direction of the price, especially using a method devised by John Hayden and explained in his book 'RSI: the complete guide'.

John Hayden explains in this text that the real levels that measure the strength of the bullish or bearish trend are not the standard ones, i.e. 30 and 70, but are actually 33.33 and 66.66. Even if these values do not differ much from the values indicated by Wilder, it seems that they can give better indications than the classic ones. A market that fails to reach the 66.66 threshold is a weak market, while a market that fails to break below the 33.33 threshold is a strong market.

In the picture below you can find an example of the RSI indicator adjusted to meet Hayden's standards. The chart refers to Aave, one of the most important cryptocurrencies in the DeFi space.

Chapter 5 - MACD

MACD is one of the best known technical analysis tools and is considered by many to be a real trading system.

The construction of this indicator is quite simple. In fact, it is based on two moving averages, which certainly are the most used chart tool by technical analysts for their simplicity as we have seen in previous chapters. In other chapters we have seen how the crossing of two moving averages, whether simple or exponential, can be used to generate trading signals. Furthermore, we have reminded you a lot of times to always take into account the limits of this system.

We have also highlighted how moving averages react differently depending on the time domain to which they refer. In fact, the shorter the average, the more reactive it will be, i.e. it will keep closer to prices than an average with a greater time domain.

The resulting concept is quite simple. A short average will be useful to signal the presence of a short-term trend while a longer average will signal the existence of the underlying trend.

The next step, i.e. the simultaneous use of the two averages, will tell us whether the short trend (short average) is confirmed by the underlying trend (long average). The intersection of the two moving averages of different time domains indicates the change in the trend. In fact, the short average, which is more reactive than the long one, will react first to the change in trend and will cross the longer-term average upwards or downwards.

A bullish crossing, which occurs when the shorter average crosses the longer average from bottom to top, leads to suspect the birth of an upward trend. We will then have further confirmation of the reliability of the current trend when even the average of the largest temporal domain will be oriented upwards. When choosing the two averages, it must be borne in mind that the greater the time domain used, the lower the number of signals generated. Conversely, the smaller the domain and the greater the amount of trading indications provided by the system. In this case, the price to pay will be given by the increase in false signals.

The ease of use of moving averages has facilitated the creation and dissemination of a series of indicators for their implementation. MACD, an acronym for Moving Average Convergence-Divergence, is certainly one of the most well-known trend-following indicators.

This indicator was created by Gerald Appel with the aim of representing the interaction of two exponential moving averages of a predetermined time domain: 12 and 26 periods. The strength of this indicator is undoubtedly represented by its high popularity. It is intuitive that the more traders use it, the greater its reliability. The weak point, on the other hand, is represented by the fact that predetermined parameters are suitable for identifying only that market cycle that is based only on those same parameters.

Of course, the parameters can be changed at will, but in this case we would sacrifice the first strength (that of the reliability due to the wide use of the indicator with the default parameters among traders).

How to set the MACD indicator

The MACD is based on the operating principle that we have already highlighted. The fast average will record the change in price directions before the slow one and the crossing on the longer-term one should identify the start of a trend. This signal will be all the more reliable the faster the slower average will orient itself in the same way as the faster one.

Since the MACD is based on the difference between an average of 12 and an average of 26 periods, the crossing will have occurred when the value of the indicator is zero. Above the zero line the trend can be qualified as bullish and vice versa.

The picture below should give you a better understanding of what we are talking about.

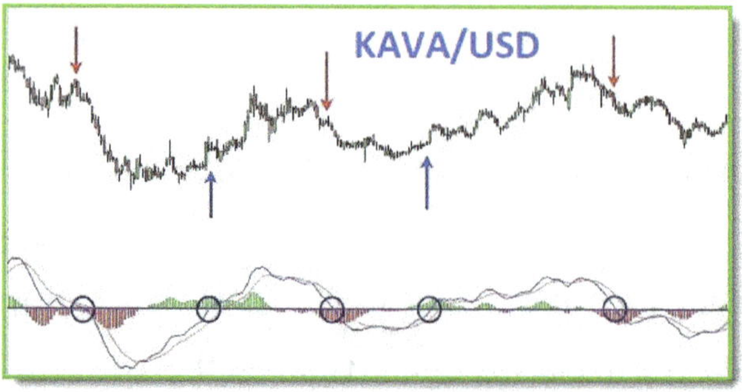

Therefore, the zero line is of great importance because it allows the trader to immediately detect the moment of crossing of the two averages.

In the indicator there is also another line, called the signal line, obtained from the nine-period average of the MACD, which in the indicator shown in the graph above we see highlighted in red.

The signal line has an anticipatory function of the crossing of the zero line and, in many cases, allows you to correctly anticipate the market entry with respect to the beginning of the trend. The signal in this case occurs when the MACD (blue line) crosses the signal line (red line).

At the same instant, the histogram in the indicator crosses the zero line, facilitating the identification of the intersection between the MACD and its signal line.

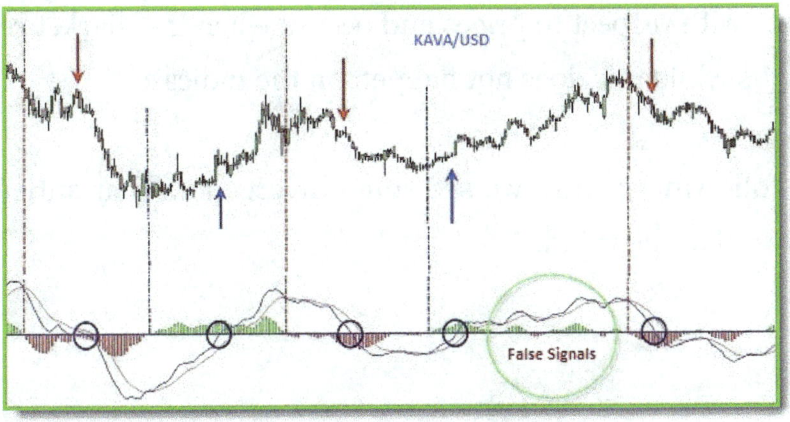

Therefore, in the image above we see a comparison of the classic entry given by the crossing of the zero line by the MACD (indicated by the blue and red arrows) with the entry based on the crossing of the signal line with the line MACD (indicated by dashed lines).

Obviously, as often happens when trying to 'anticipate' the market, here too there is no lack of false signals, as highlighted in the area circled in green. But it is clear that early entry often turns out to be a winner.

How to take advantage of the MACD for your trading strategy

Another very common and effective use of this indicator is to detect divergences with prices. We have already spoken several times about the divergences. A divergence is a different trend of the indicator with respect to prices and occurs when the market records new highs while this does not happen on the indicator.

In the following picture we see some divergences that anticipated the reversal of the trend.

The blue arrow indicates a first long-term divergence that marks the reversal of the trend from bearish to bullish. A subsequent bearish divergence, indicated by the red arrow, warns us of the beginning of a bearish correction of some importance (the cryptocurrency goes from 1.3 to 0.87 dollars in the space of a single month).

As you can see in the graphs shown, the MACD indicator is also composed of a histogram represented in green if it is above the zero line, in red if it is below. This histogram represents the difference between the MACD line value and the signal line.

This component can also provide interesting insights to support us in reading the price trend. When the range of the histogram becomes smaller and smaller, that is, it gets closer and closer to the zero line, it means that we have low volatility. In fact, the price is moving in the trading range and is ready to explode in a certain direction.

This particular trend of the MACD histogram is called 'histogram squeeze'. So let's see how to exploit this particular conformation to intercept a valid breakout. In the following picture (the coin we are considering is Ethereum, ticker symbol ETH) we see the prices that move in an uptrend and in the last part they generate a correction in the shape of a flag.

If we look at the MACD histogram in the panel below the prices, we notice that, as the price falls, the histogram becomes smaller and smaller, even creating a bullish divergence.

This loss of momentum may indicate that prices are consolidating and are ready to explode again in the direction of the current trend (which in this case is bullish).

Indeed, in the last bearish movement that tests the lower side of the flag, the histogram remains in positive territory and, as soon as prices touch the lower side of the flag, they turn violently upwards. In this case, the MACD line also generates a bullish divergence. The validity of the upper side breakout is confirmed by the MACD histogram in positive territory and with high values.

As we have seen, the use of MACD goes far beyond the classic indicators we are used to seeing in the various chapters on this book.

Knowing in depth its possible applications, the MACD can provide us with considerable support in our decision-making process. It could be a very useful suggestion to decide whether to open a position in a certain direction rather than in the opposite one.

Therefore, it is no coincidence that the MACD is among the indicators most used by cryptocurrency traders. In particular, it works pretty well with DeFi related cryptocurrencies like Ethereum, Aave, Kava and RLC.

Chapter 6 - Bollinger Bands

John Bollinger certainly needs no introduction. He is responsible for many of the insights that can fully enter our ideal encyclopedia of technical analysis. To him, among others, we owe the creation of the famous "bands" that bear his name and of which we are going to discuss in this chapter.

To fully understand the usefulness of Bollinger bands, it is appropriate to take a small step back. In a previous chapter we talked about moving averages and we saw that this tool, perhaps the first and simplest with which the novice trader finds themselves tinkering, is graphed according to the "history" of prices. The moving average tends to position below prices in an uptrend and above them in downtrends.

Let's see an example on the Bitcoin chart with a simple moving average of 20 periods per hour. Do not be surprised by the dollar amount, we are going back to the early days for this chapter.

From the simple moving average we moved on to the construction of the so-called envelopes or bands in an attempt to "cage" prices. We wanted to create a dynamic channel that follows the trend of prices. The bands are obtained thanks to two averages constructed by moving a moving average of a given time domain up and down by a percentage at will. In the following graph we see the bands applied to the 20-period central moving average of the previous example, with a vertical shift of 1.5%.

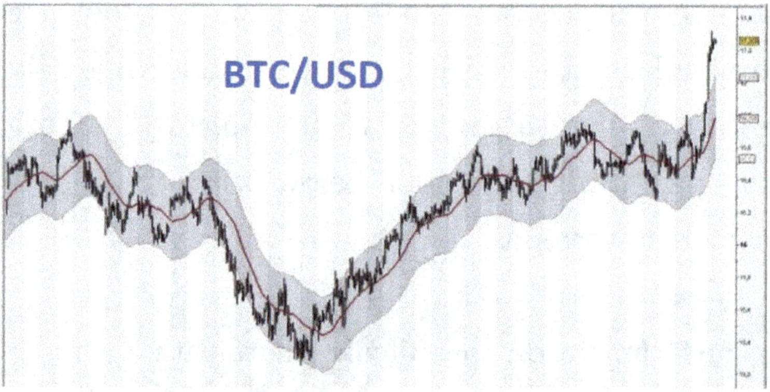

As we can see, the bands create a typical channel that indicates a range where it is easy to determine whether the price is overbought or oversold.

In particular, the lower part of the channel thus obtained can be considered a support while the upper part, on the contrary, can be considered as a resistance.

The limit of this analysis tool is the value of the percentage that defines the width of the channel. In fact, this value does not take into account the conditions of volatility, or the sudden moments of acceleration in prices with respect to the lateral phases or market congestion.
In fact, in the previous chart we can see that during the last phase of acceleration the bands were unable to contain prices. Therefore, the contact with the upper bands gave rise to a false signal, while up to that moment the bands had been able to contain the price trend.

The Bollinger Bands remedy the problem highlighted above since, taking into account the volatility in the period under consideration, they are able to better adapt to the price trend in any market condition, automatically adjusting the width of the channel accordingly. The greater or lesser volatility of the moment, the broader or narrower the channel.

In the picture below, we can see the same chart with the application of the Bollinger Bands.

In the chart above, the old bands are red while the band delimited by the Bollinger Bands is blue. It is evident that the new bands better adapt to the price trend compared to the previous ones.

This is a consequence, as mentioned, of the construction criteria of the bands which causes them to widen in the periods in which the price range is wider and that they shrink in the moments of laterality.

The trader thus has an immediate perception of how market volatility is evolving. In fact, from an operational point of view, the narrowing of the bands, consequent to the decrease in volatility, could be a prelude to sudden directional movements, an explosion of volatility. Therefore, we can assume the opening of buying positions when prices pierce the lower band.

Similarly, the break of the upper band can be adopted for the opening of a short position.

To eliminate some of the false signals that such a system can inevitably generate, it is advisable to adopt one or more confirmation filters, such as an oscillator that is suitable for identify, in conjunction with the signal provided by the Bollinger Bands, overbought or oversold areas, preferably associated with a divergence. The Relative Strength Index is a perfect complementary indicator to the Bollinger Bands and oftentimes these two are used together to maximize the accuracy of the predictions.

Chapter 7 - Fibonacci

For those that have had previous experience with trading cryptocurrencies or other financial assets, Fibonacci should be a very well known tool. In fact, it is probably one of the most used tools to analyze charts, price retracements and identify new targets.

This chapter is going to tell you everything you need to know about this fascinating tool and how to apply it to your trading strategies.

Fibonacci retracements are a technical analysis tool that uses percentages and horizontal lines drawn on price charts to identify possible areas of support and resistance.

Markets generally do not move along straight lines, but are characterized by oscillatory movements around a trend line. These swings are nothing more than temporary price movements that go against the direction of the main trend and are known as pull backs or retracements.

Fibonacci retracements allow us to identify possible areas where prices can find temporary support or resistance. The levels of this indicator are based on the mathematical principle of the golden ratio discovered by the Tuscan mathematician Leonardo Pisano, called Fibonacci.

The sequence for the golden ratio is 0, 1, 1, 2, 3, 5, 8, 13, 21, 34, 55, 89, 144, and so on, where each number is the sum of the two numbers preceding it. According to the golden ratio, a series of percentage values are identified that could indicate support and resistance levels.

The best known levels - and which you will find by default on every trading platform like Tradingview - are: 23.6%, 38.2%, 50%, 61.8% and 100%. There are also other levels, less known such as 76.4%. However, almost all platforms nowadays allow you to set custom levels on the charts.

An image can help clarify doubts. From the image below you can see the daily chart of the ADA/USD exchange rate during a descending phase (ADA is the ticker symbol of Cardano). The trend is therefore bearish, i.e. inclined downwards, and the exchange rate went from 1.24 to 1.15 in the space of a few weeks. By setting the Fibonacci indicator to the maximum and dragging it to the minimum, all the Fibonacci retracements appear. A trader can thus identify the areas where the exchange can find resistance in the rebound phase and, therefore, where sales could restart.

In the present case, on the second retracement (38.2%) it can be observed how prices find resistance and sales break down with strength (red candle).

We could say that Fibonacci retracements are used by traders to identify the degree to which a market will move against its main trend. Going back to the example above, the rebound could have been more important and also point to 50% or 61.8%. Normally, if the market retraces more than 61.8%, the trend could be at risk of reversal. So there is a tendency to give a lot of importance to this last level. In most cases, the retracement ranges from 23.6% to 38.2%.

The identification of these areas is useful for traders as it can help them decide when to open, as well as indicate possible stops and limits for their operations.

The example above takes into consideration a bearish trend. Obviously the same is true in the case of an uptrend. In this second case, the Fibonacci levels will constitute interesting supports on which it is possible to operate in the event of a pull back.

How to use Fibonacci in trading?

We have already mentioned that Fibonacci levels tell traders when it is the right time to open or close a position. So Fibonacci retracements can be very effective when used correctly. However, these require a high level of understanding to be used effectively. Simply drawing lines on a price chart at Fibonacci percentages will likely not yield positive results unless traders know what they are looking for. Consequently, novice traders should be careful when using Fibonacci retracements to be sure that a drop in the price of an asset is a temporary pull back and not a permanent reversal.

Some traders believe that Fibonacci retracements are a self-fulfilling prophecy. In fact, as many traders use Fibonacci retracements as a technical analysis tool, they are likely to get the same results. This means that orders tend to congregate around the same price levels, which could push the price in the desired direction. This thesis is partly true, although many traders today use multiple indicators before making an operational decision.

The best Fibonacci trading strategies

We see below some of the Fibonacci strategies among the most used, namely the mild, deep and medium retracement.

Mild retracement

Normally a slight pull back is what goes from 23.6% to 38.2%. They are among the most frequent that can be found in the cryptocurrency markets. However, there are also less profound retracements. These retracements generally occur when a market is trending with strength. In these cases, pull backs are usually very mild and mostly identify a consolidation phase. These situations require a strong skill to be exploited as the market moves quickly. Therefore, entering a strongly trending market can be not easy for many traders, since a stop loss must also be set. Generally, it would make sense to set the stop loss below the previous swing low in a bull market or above the previous swing high in a bear market.

It should also be added that when a market is in a strong trend, traders often come into play without considering the risk-return profile or the use of the stop loss. However, it makes sense to enter during the consolidation of a strong trending market, as this consolidation will often represent a continuation pause of the main trend.

Deep retracement

The search for entry positions within deeper Fibonacci retracements is another widely used trading strategy, especially by more speculative traders. The trading opportunities in this case occur with significant market pullbacks, which even exceed the level of 61.8%. Compared to mild retracements, the latter tend to occur in more mature trends and not in strong acceleration as those in the initial phase can be.

It is logical to think that the deeper retracements occur at points where there are many divergent opinions among traders with a prevalence of traders starting to be skeptical about the continuation of the trend.

Medium retracement

There are also retracements in the middle between the slight and deep ones, called medium retracements. They are usually less frequent than mild retracements and are characterized by pullbacks ranging between 38.2% and 61.8%. Generally they have a well-defined trend, but which has not yet exhausted its initial strength.

Fibonacci Extensions

For the sake of completeness, let's close with a brief mention of Fibonacci extensions. If retracements are usually used as a market entry level, extensions are ideal for determining profit levels, where the position can be closed.

In fact, the extensions represent the levels that the market can reach once it has retraced and is about to restart in the same direction as the main trend. Therefore, they identify the levels that they target once the trend has been broken down.

There are several extension levels: 127.2%, 138.2%, 161.8%, 261.8% and 423.6%, although the most common ones are 138.2, 161.8 and 261.8%. As with retracements, it is possible to enter customized levels in the various trading platforms.

Chapter 8 - Stochastic Relative Strength Index

This oscillator evaluates how close the closures of the bars are to the maximum or minimum recorded in a certain period (by default in the most popular trading platforms, like Tradingview, we find a period of 14 bars).

The inventor's intuition consists in having understood that, as a rule, bar closings close to their maximum are typical of upward trends, while bar closings towards the minimum are indicative of a bearish trend.

We do not go into the details of the oscillator calculation as now all analysis software foresees its construction. It is suffice to say that the original calculation is based on the current value compared to the minimum and maximum values of the price recorded in a certain period. This gives rise to a defined value %K from which its defined average %D is then determined.

The different types of stochastic - strengths and weaknesses

There are three versions of Stochastic. The fast stochastic represents the original formula in which the %K line is obtained by relating the closing price and a certain price range (at 14 periods) as a percentage, while the %D line is simply the average mobile (normally 3 periods) of the %K line.

However, the so-called stochastic fast has the drawback of being too reactive and difficult to apply. To overcome this problem, a variant has been created which generates better interpretable signals and which is defined as low stochastic. In this version of the stochastic the %K line is constructed as a moving average (3 periods) of the %D line of the fast stochastic version, while the %D line represents in turn the moving average (3 periods) of the new %K line.

Then there is a version that is called full stochastic which is a customizable variant of the slow stochastic. In this latest version we can set all the necessary parameters. We can set the number of periods to be taken into consideration, the number of periods for the %K and the number of periods for the %D. This latest version is the one most used by most traders.

How the stochastic is interpreted

The stochastic is an oscillator and therefore moves or 'fluctuates' between the values 0 and 100. No matter how much the price of the cryptocurrency moves down or up, the stochastic will always fluctuate between the values 0 and 100. One of the more elementary uses of the stochastic is to identify areas of excess prices, or the so-called oversold when we have values below 20 and the so-called overbought when these values exceed the value 80. Obviously you can vary these values at will to adapt them to the cryptocurrency on which you are operating.

It is correct to underline that if prices are in the overbought and oversold areas, you should not necessarily expect a trend reversal, nor the reversal will be immediate. Often, in fact, the stochastic enters the overbought and oversold area in situations of sustained and well-defined trends and the oscillator remains in these areas for a long time without ever crossing the 80-20 dividing line. This is why it is good to be very careful not to use this oscillator to automatically capture signals against the trend.

Conversely, this oscillator is great for generating signals during sideways phases.

Stochastic use in an undefined trend

Let's first begin to see what the classic use of the stochastic is.

Below is the chart of Bitcoin in a descending lateral phase. The thing that leads us to think that the cryptocurrency is entering a lateral phase are the first 4 overlapping movements. In fact, we do not have a linear movement in a single direction, but a continuous overlapping of movements. Once we have identified two points on the top and two points on the bottom, we can trace our two trend lines and then project them forward.

Our operations include the purchase of the cryptocurrency every time the price touches the lower trend line and the two stochastic lines cross in the oversold area.

Conversely, we will sell whenever the price touches the upper trend line and the two stochastic lines cross in the overbought zone. We will avoid taking a stand if the two conditions do not occur at the same time.

In the second part of this chapter on the stochastic we will see how to best use it in a well-defined trend phase, as well as how to exploit the signals deriving from the so-called divergences between price and oscillator.

Use of the stochastic oscillator in a trending market

We have seen how the Stochastic oscillator is very effective and able to generate excellent trading signals not only in the lateral phases, where the prices move from a static support to a resistance, but also in the phases of moderate price trend.

Instead, it is rather risky to use the stochastic to operate against the trend, or when the instrument considered shows a good trend, bullish or bearish.

Therefore, if you want to use this oscillator in the trend phases, you must wait for the development of a well-defined trend, then a subsequent retracement and take advantage of the stochastic to enter the direction of the original trend, trying to capture the end of the correction.

An operational advice to reduce the number of false signals is to set your oscillator using parameters 20-5-5 instead of those 14-3-3 proposed by default by the graphical analysis platforms like Tradingview.

Of course, even in this case, the advice remains to carry out in-depth tests to evaluate which, in the past, were the best settings of the indicator capable of returning the least possible number of false signals.

The stochastic at work to capture the restarts of the trend

The following is a 15-minute chart of the ETH/USD price chart. The index implements a fairly significant first bearish movement, so much so that we assume that the current trend will continue in the same original direction after a correction.

The stochastic confirms the strong bearish trend underway as it enters the oversold area and tends to stay there for a long time. On the subsequent price rebound, we wait for the oscillator to rise and enter the overbought zone. At the same time, we can see that ETH fails to retrace 50% of the first bearish movement, an evident sign of weakness.

The short signal is generated when the two stochastic lines cross in the overbought area; a condition that indicates the correction as potentially terminated (area circled in red in the graph).

It is essential to take into consideration a well-defined trend, as in this case there is a very good chance that, after the correction, the trend will resume its original direction.
It is precisely the stochastic that signals the strength of the current trend, remaining for a long time in the oversold area in the event of a bearish trend, as we see in the previous graph, or in the overbought area, in the case of an uptrend.

Operations in divergence

Another type of trading with the stochastic involves the identification of divergences between prices and the oscillator as a filter to open the position. The divergences on the oscillator occur quite often and are generally quite reliable when associated with other trading signals. Let's see also in this case a practical example.

Below we see an hourly chart of the Uniswap price chart against the dollar.

As we can see in the descent that achieves the absolute minimum on the chart, the price generates two decreasing lows at which the stochastic oscillator realizes, on the contrary, two increasing lows. The above is a classic case of bullish divergence in which, as we can see from the chart, the cryptocurrency reversed the trend.

It is preferable to use the divergences on movements with a moderate trend in the absence of a trend (lateral phases) as the probability of success of the operation is higher. On the contrary, with cryptocurrencies in strong trend we could see multiple divergences before there is an actual trend reversal, with several inevitable false signals.

Also for this reason it is advisable to use the divergences not as a real signal of entry into position, but as a confirmation filter to be associated with other techniques that directly exploit the relationships between prices.

Chapter 9 - Head and Shoulders

The head and shoulders is one of the most reliable inversion patterns in technical analysis. Being a reversal figure, it is assumed that this pattern occurs after a prolonged trend, bullish or bearish. The completion of the figure is a prelude to the immediate reversal of the current trend.

Let's see an example of a head and shoulders.

What we see in the image is a bearish head and shoulders, a formation of technical analysis which reverses the current upward trend. The following considerations mirror the bullish head and shoulders.

The bearish head and shoulders, as we see in the picture, is made up of three consecutive highs among which the highest is the central one, basically three bullish tears that each form a maximum: the first two rising and the third decreasing with respect to the second.

With the first rise, the formation of the first maximum and the subsequent correction, the “left shoulder” is graphically delineated. After the correction, a new bullish break takes place which culminates in a higher high than the previous one, followed by a new correction. This movement gives rise to the formation of the so-called "head".

We can have the first signs of a head and shoulders in formation from the divergence on the volumes, if these are higher on the left shoulder than the head. In fact, we know that a trend, to be healthy, must be accompanied by volumes and the formation of a new maximum ("head") with decreasing volumes compared to the previous maximum ("left shoulder") warns us of a possible deterioration of the current trend.

Finally we have a third bullish break, with the formation of a lower maximum than the previous one and once again a correction to test the trendline that unites the minimums of the formation and which, in practice, delimits the corrections we have seen so far. This trendline, which takes the name of "neckline", is extremely important because it is with its downward violation that the head and shoulders pattern is completed. The increase in trading volumes, on the occasion of the break of the neckline, increases the probability of success for the head and shoulders.

After the breaking of the neckline, we often witness a return of the prices to test the same neckline from the bottom up, as we can see in the previous image. This rebound must necessarily occur with decreasing volumes, confirming that it is simple profit taking by operators due to the closure of short positions, and not the resumption of the upward trend. The confirmation of the movement takes place with the neckline test and the resumption of the fall in prices.

Let's now see the diagram shown in the previous image on a real chart.

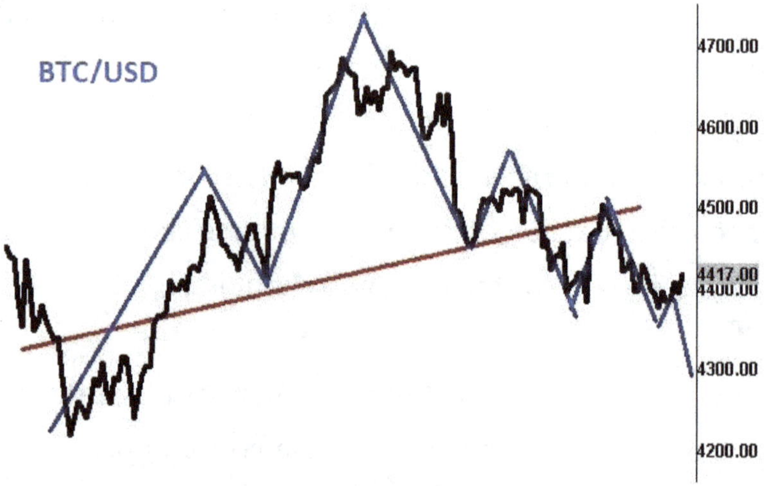

As can be seen from this chart, in the real market it is necessary to have the ability to identify the pattern that does not always develop according to canonical criteria. In the above case, for example, we have a "head" made up of two maxima (a double top, to be exact). Very often, then, the two shoulders (left and right) do not have the same extension, as in the case depicted.

It remains to be said of the hypothetical target for this pattern, that is the level on which we can expect the price projection once the pattern is confirmed. The technique to be used is to project the height of the pattern, measured with a perpendicular from the highest maximum up to the neckline, and project it downwards at the breaking point of the neckline itself.

In the previous case we will have the following hypothesis.

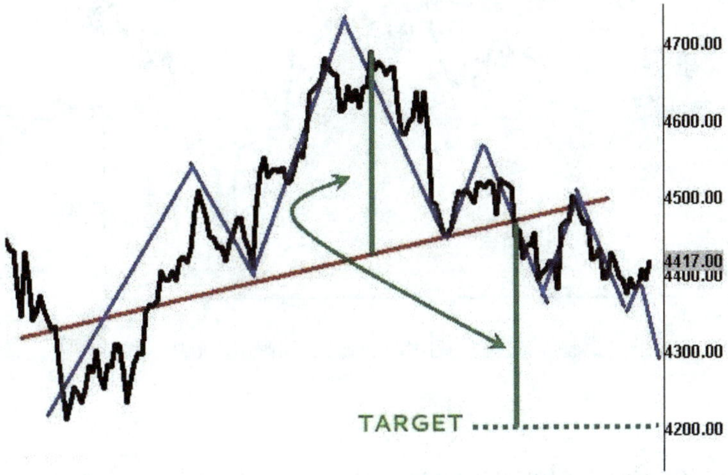

Finally, in the next image, a bullish head and shoulders on the DOT/USD chart. In this case, note the absence of the pullback and the very strong increase in volumes on the occasion of the bullish break of the neckline.

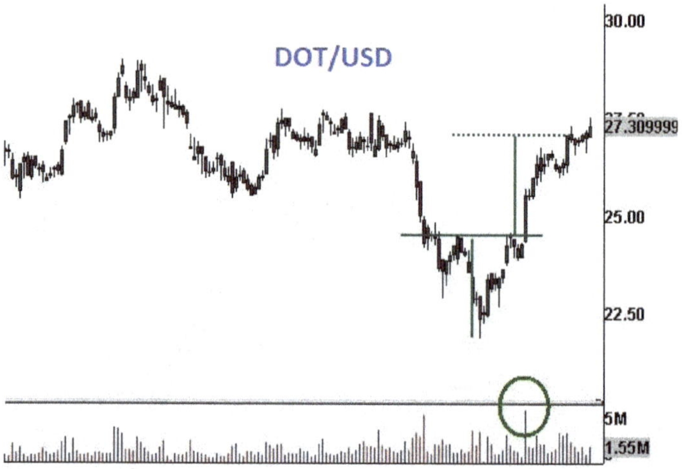

While the second elevation is the most solid and represents the head, the first and third represent the shoulders and are less accentuated than the head and almost never have the same extension. The completion of the pattern is obtained by drilling the line, joining the two reaction lows, called the "neckline". This drilling must take place with a conspicuous increase in trading volumes. Generally, after the break of the neckline there is a return of the prices towards the head, concluding with the continuation of the trend in the same direction as the break.

At least two important signals can be identified. Firstly, the break occurred during the downturn that formed the head of the uptrend line and, secondly, the confirmation with the second shoulder of the inability of the trend to reach new highs. The upward movement can be considered virtually exhausted and the bullish positions should be closed.

Chapter 10 - Price Ranges

The trading range is an area bounded by a support line (lower) and a resistance line (upper). We can also classify this chart conformation with the term of rectangle.

The price fluctuates for a long time between two static trend lines, one lower for support and one higher for resistance, forming distribution areas - if the pattern is formed at the peak of an uptrend - or accumulation areas - when the pattern occurs after a prolonged down trend.

Once the distribution or accumulation phase is completed, the price breaks one of the two sides, creating what is commonly called a breakout.

To calculate the target potential after the breakout of one of the two static trend lines, it is necessary to measure the width of the rectangle and project it from the breaking point, as we can see in the following picture.

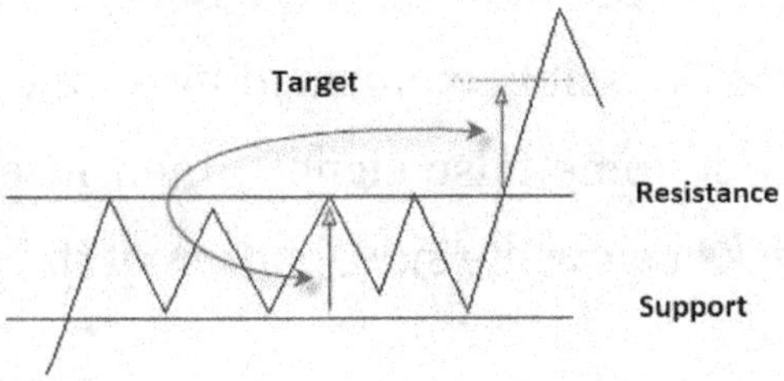

This pattern can be an inversion or a continuation of the current trend. To understand if the breakout can be more or less valid, a study of the trend of the volumes can be carried out.

Volumes should contract during the formation of the pattern and then expand at the time of the break out. Therefore, breakouts without increasing volumes (with respect to the formation phase of the pattern) could provide false signals.

Again, it is possible to observe the volumes during the formation of the pattern. In fact, volumes that expand as the price moves towards the top of the pattern can suggest a breakout of the top and vice versa. Breakouts that are confirmed by an increase in volume provide more important and reliable signals.

But let's see how these patterns can be exploited from an operational point of view, starting with the bullish breakout. The most common operational exploitation of this pattern consists in positioning long on the market at the breakout of the upper side of the trading range, possibly confirmed by an increase in volumes, in order to filter out some false signals, then inserting a stop loss to protect a few ticks below the side. bottom of the pattern.

A more conservative, and more prudent entry that allows you to significantly decrease the extent of the stop and also avoid some false signals, consists in waiting for the formation of a pullback after the breakout. Often, in fact, the price after having accelerated in the direction of the breakout, goes back to test the "old" resistance trendline, which has now become support, and then returns to rise.

Therefore, we can position ourselves long on the market after the pullback, placing the stop loss just below the pattern used as a reversal to enter the position. In this way we optimize the entry and decrease the amount of the stop. The only drawback to take into consideration is that we do not always see the formation of the pullback and using this more conservative method, it could sometimes happen that you are unable to enter the position.

Obviously, the exact opposite applies to the bearish signal (short).

Let's see some real examples to better understand this pattern.

The chart below shows a long phase of accumulation of the Polkadot chart. Here, prices break the resistance, pull back on the new support and then start to rise again to perfectly reach the target which is exactly the projection of the amplitude of the trading range.

In this case the volumes do not confirm the pattern, but we had a "textbook" pullback.

Once the trading range has been identified you can try to buy on the test of the first minimum which acts as a support, thus anticipating the classic entry point. In this case we can identify a first target already at the test of the previous resistance (upper trendline) and then aim for more ambitious targets once the bullish breakout of the figure is confirmed.

This is obviously a very aggressive way of operating, which however allows us to reduce the stop loss to a minimum which, in this case, could be positioned a few ticks below the support line, which is a very short distance from our entry point.

Chapter 11 - How to Use Breakouts to Maximize Your Profits

The term breakout is certainly one of the best known even among trading newbies because it is often used by analysts to indicate the possibility for the prices of the given cryptocurrency to be able to give rise to a strongly directional movement when a certain level is exceeded.

The term breakout is precisely to identify the violation of a certain level, normally of support or resistance, from which to expect a strong movement of prices in the same direction as the break. So if prices come from the bottom and break a major resistance, this breakout can give rise to a bullish directional move. On the contrary, if prices come from above and go to breach a support level, a bearish directional movement is often expected.

Let's see a practical example.

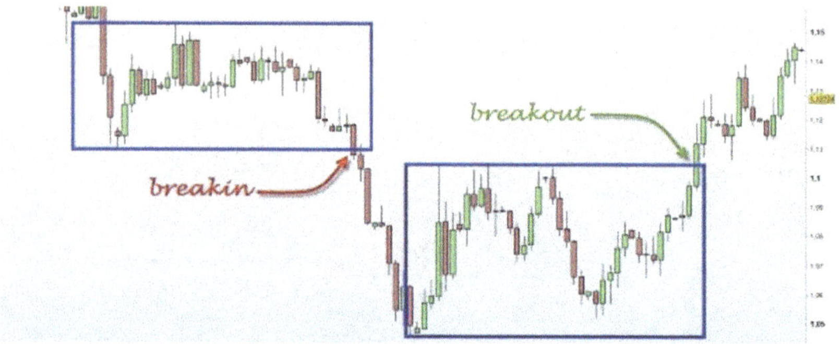

In the left box we see how the break of the support (breakin) has led to a strong bearish acceleration while, in the second box, the breakout of the highs tested several times (resistance) has given rise to a rather prolonged rise.

As we have been able to verify in the example above, truly effective breakouts often occur after rather prolonged periods of laterality (price congestion). These are phases of the market without real directionality in which the uncertainty of operators about the future movement of prices prevails. In these cases a real battle is unleashed between two opposing armies, that of the buyers who accumulate the financial instrument in question trusting in a subsequent price increase and that of the sellers who, conversely, operate a distribution (i.e. sell) expecting a subsequent discount. The breaking of the levels that are thus formed, commonly called resistances and supports, gives rise to a real acceleration of prices which, substantially, derives from the fact that the market now seems to have taken a direction, putting an end to the lateral phase.

Subsequent falls, in the event of a breakin, or the rises, in the event of a breakout, are often a consequence of new sales (or new purchases) that feed themselves. In fact, as traders witness the formation of long bullish or bearish candles they enter the market in the same direction, strengthening and confirming the breach of the support or resistance level.

These are often explosive movements because they are also fueled by the closure of the positions of those who, in the lateral phase, had positioned themselves on the wrong side of the market. This is why, very often, the leaking of prices from these particular technical patterns is violent and the trends that follow are particularly consistent.

In other words, after a period of low volatility that squeezes prices between a support level and a resistance level, at the break of one of the two levels, prices show a strong acceleration in the direction of the breach.

To better understand the idea, we can think of the lateral phase as a spring that is compressed and which, once released, puts an end to the situation of compression of prices that explode in one or the other direction (upward or downward).

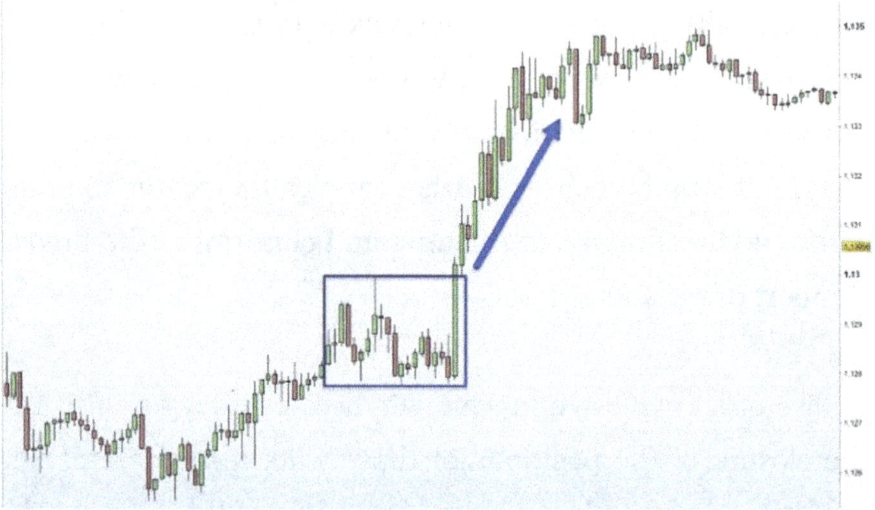

Notice in the chart above how an important trend was followed at the breakout, validated by a strong volatility expansion candle. The graph is representative of the classic situation that gives rise to the breakout. In fact, first price rise, followed by a phase of congestion (blue rectangle) and then the exit of the prices breakout in the same direction of origin.

Obviously, not all breakouts work the same way. Indeed, sometimes they do not work at all, giving rise to those patterns known with the term "false breakout", "bull trap" or "bear trap"

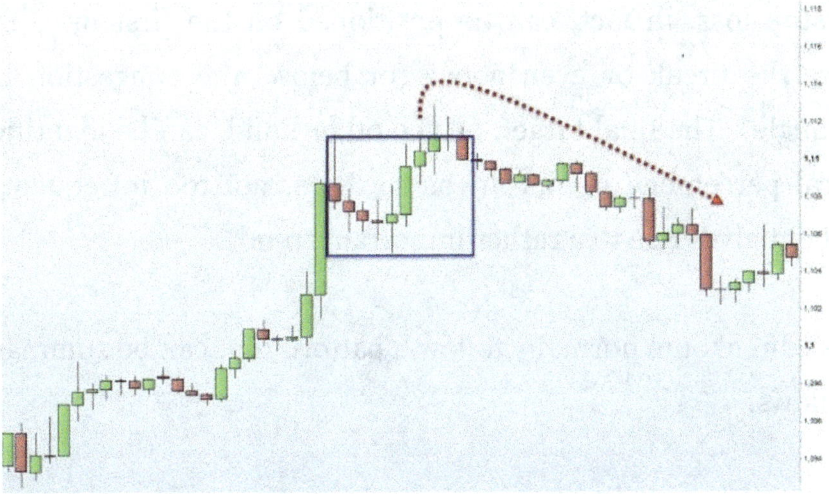

In the chart above we see a classic case of a failed breakout. Prices twice break the previous highs, suggesting a continuation of the uptrend, but immediately afterwards they fall into congestion giving rise to a real trend inversion.

Personally we are rather wary of the breakouts that we deal with very particular techniques, but it must be said that systems based on this particular price configuration are normally considered among the safest and most profitable by most traders. This, on the one hand, because they are easily identifiable (a break in a support or a resistance is a rather objective data) and, on the other hand, because they can be treated with a rather limited risk compared to the high potential they have.

The stop loss, in fact, can be positioned on the first price swing before the break or even above (or below) the congestion levels (rectangle). The final target, on the other hand, can be identified in several percentage points in cases where, not too infrequent, the breakout gives rise to a rather important trend.

Classic breakouts normally follow a pattern that can be summarized as follows.

- lateral movement that delimits the lower (support) and upper (resistance) levels that enclose the price movement;
- price violation of one of the two levels;
- development of movement in the direction of the trend. Sometimes, this is preceded by a quick retracement towards the level previously violated (so-called pullback)

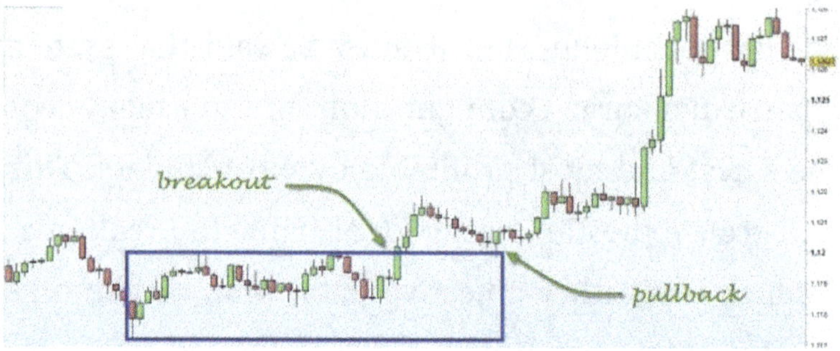

In the image above we see the classic pullback that follows the breakout, or the return of prices to the previous violated level, in this case to the upside (but the reverse is true for the breakin).

The pullback is often due to the profit taking of some operators and the sales of those traders who are not very careful or not convinced of the validity of the break. One of the systems for filtering false breakouts is precisely to operate not on the first break but to wait for the pullback or even the return of prices within the rectangle.

In this case, as we see in the detail of chart 5, the position can be opened once prices should again go above (or below) the resistance level (or support) formed after the first breakout.

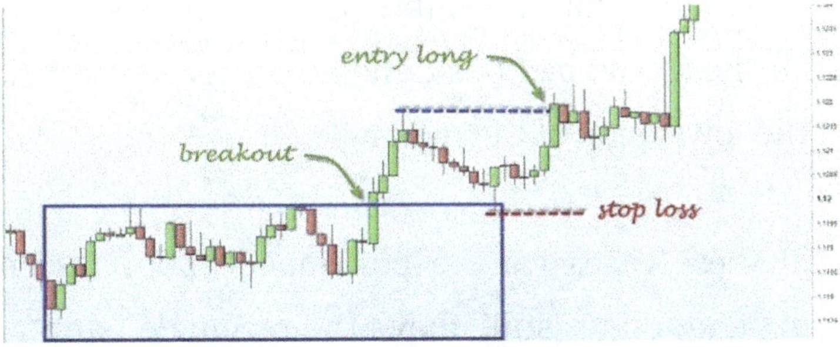

Obviously, you run the risk of losing all those price movements which, once the breakout occurs, immediately make directional movements without giving rise to a pullback.

Let's see a similar example on a breakin. Check out the image below.

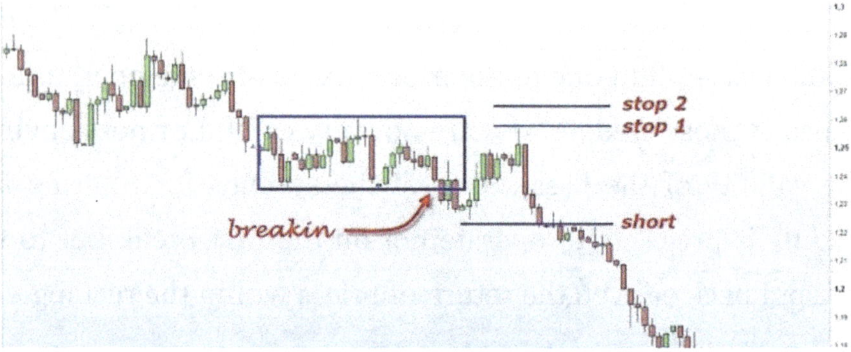

Also in this case we see how waiting for the pullback before opening the bearish position is rewarding. In fact, not only do the prices fall within the rectangle, but the pullback is so deep that this situation would have created many doubts about the goodness of the operation for those who had positioned themselves short at the first breakin of the lower side of the rectangle.

The stop in these cases can be positioned above the maximum swing (stop1) and, better still, above the rectangle (stop 2). This is the rule that we normally follow when the retracement is so deep as to physiologically reduce the amplitude of the stop loss.

In this regard it must be said that often the stop loss is so large as to advise against the operation because the risk would be too high.

Obviously, in such cases all that is wise to do is to carefully avoid taking a stand.

A different entry technique, to minimize the extent of the stop loss, especially if operating on high time frames, is the one we use when looking for a subsequent or concurrent pattern to the pullback, as long as it is in the direction of the break.

In other words, if there is a breakout, we await a bullish pattern (hammer, bullish engulfing or other) that forms at the same time as the breakout or immediately after it. Our entry level, in the event of a breakout, will be at the break of the high of the benchmark candle with a stop immediately below the candle itself (or the low of the pattern in the case of a multi-candlestick pattern such as in the case of bullish engulfing). The opposite is true for bearish scenarios..

Let's see what we mean in the chart below.

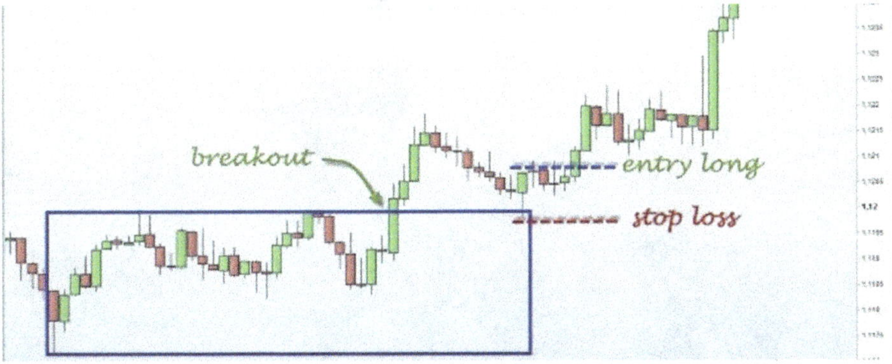

This method allows you to limit the risk that is identified in the range of the benchmark candle even if it may happen that the market still hesitates before restarting, going to touch the minimum of the benchmark candle and sweeping away the stop. Precisely for this reason, the advice is not to place the stop too close to the low of the candle to give the operation a little more breathing space.

Chapter 12 - Support and Resistance Levels

In many different chapters we have used the terms support and resistance. While their meaning should be clear by now, we feel it is our responsibility to give you a complete explanation of these two concepts. In fact, they are an incredible tool at your disposal to anticipate market movements.

We can imagine support and resistance as a floor and ceiling limiting the range of movement of the market. Understanding these important technical analysis concepts will help you develop a disciplined and efficient trading strategy.

The dynamism and volatility of prices on the market are the result of the continuous variation of the balance between supply and demand. When supply exceeds demand, prices tend to fall. Vice versa when supply is not sufficient to satisfy demand, prices tend to rise.

Technical analysts identify trends in the markets by studying the price levels at which the balances change. Although these levels are created in a completely natural way, without following any program, they represent the collective opinion of the subjects operating on the market.

Support level

Support is the level at which a bearish price stops falling and potentially 'bounces' back up.

This is because potential buyers, given the fall in the price, decide it is a good time to enter the market. The excess supply is then absorbed, until supply and demand are rebalanced and the decline stops. As the number of buyers increases, the balance tilts again towards demand and prices start to rise again.

Technical analysts can identify plausible support levels, but without any guarantees as markets are never fully predictable. It is worth remembering that if a price breaks through the expected support level, it will continue to fall until it finds another support. In technical analysis when prices break a support we speak of a bearish breakout of a support.

Support is that price level at which there is such a concentration of demand as to oppose the fall in prices for a significant period of time.

Resistance level

Resistance is the opposite of support. It is the level at which a rising price finds resistance to growth and potentially falls.

This is because potential sellers, given the price rise, decide it's a good time to sell. This generates an increase in supply on the market, which eventually catches up with demand creating a new equilibrium. However, an increasing number of sellers are trying to take advantage of the bull market by creating a sales force that pushes prices down again.

Some technical analysts believe that a price that violates the expected resistance level can continue to rise until it reaches the next resistance. In technical analysis when prices break a resistance (upward breach) we speak of a bullish breakout of a resistance.

Resistance is that price level at which a sharp increase in sales volumes can be expected to counteract purchases, in order to hinder the rise in prices for a certain period of time.

Types of supports and resistances

We can divide the supports and resistances into the two following categories.

- Static
- Dynamic

Static supports are horizontal segments that can be drawn on strategic technical levels (such as relative and / or absolute minimums).

For example, we can consider as static supports the following things:

- absolute minimums or relative minimums;
- psychological barriers (round figures);
- Fibonacci retracements of an ascent;
- lower limit of a rectangle (lateral channel, horizontal band, box, trading range);
- pivot supports.

Static resistances are horizontal segments that can be drawn on strategic technical levels (such as relative and / or absolute maximums). For example, we can consider static resistances the following things.

- absolute maximums or relative maximums;
- psychological barriers;
- Fibonacci retracements of a descent;
- upper limit of a side channel;
- pivot resistances.

Dynamic supports are lines and curves that lie below the price line and represent an obstacle to a price drop. Unlike static supports, the values change over time.

For example, we can consider dynamic supports the following things.

- a bullish trendline;
- the lower limit of a descending channel;
- the moving averages;
- the lower limit of the Bollinger Bands;
- the neckline of a bearish head and shoulders.

Dynamic resistances are lines or curves that are located above the price line and represent an obstacle to a rise in prices. Unlike static resistances, the values change over time.

For example we can consider dynamic resistances the following things.

- a bearish trendline;
- the upper limit of an ascending channel;
- the moving averages;
- the upper limit of the Bollinger Bands;
- the neckline of a bullish head and shoulders.

"Bear" and "bull" markets

These terms are used to describe the thinking of two different groups of traders.

Bears

They are the sellers, who assume that prices are destined to go down. A "bear" market is a market where prices are declining.

Bulls

They are the buyers, who assume that prices are destined to rise. A "bull" market is a market where the prices of a single asset or security are rising.

Practical examples of supports and resistances

In a side trading range, the market is relatively stable with a limited degree of volatility, defined by the support and resistance levels. However, market conditions can change for a variety of reasons. If market conditions improve, for example, the balance between supply and demand is altered.

Here is an example of a sequence of events that can lead to a change in support and resistance.

Let's assume the company behind a certain cryptocurrency announces positive news.

Sellers (the offer) will be less likely to sell and will stick to their coins in hopes that the cryptocurrency will gain value. Buyers will instead be eager to enter the market.
As the price approaches the previous resistance level again, the number of "bears" will decrease while the number of "bulls" will increase. This allows prices to break out of the previous resistance level, creating what is commonly referred to as a 'break out' (as we have seen in the previous chapter).

However, not all bulls and bears will change their minds. Most investment news is open to interpretation, and some investors may not get the message right. These investors who have not reacted to the announcement will consolidate the upward movement of the price into a new trend. Some short sellers, who have sold the cryptocurrency to open a position, will have placed stops on the previous resistance level, in order to close the position and limit losses in the event of a price rise. When these orders are triggered by the price increase, the short sale closes with the purchase. This creates more demand and contributes to the bull market.

Other buyers who had previously decided not to participate may notice that the side range has been broken and decide to take a stand. This leads to a further increase in demand, driving prices up even more.

Conditions for a new level of support

Now the market has broken through the previous resistance level, which can become the new support level. Traders will have seen the price take a big leap forward after breaking the resistance and may decide to buy the cryptocurrency if the price returns to this level. The reasons could be due to emotional responses such as the following.

Fear of the market

Short sellers who had opened a position just below the resistance level, expecting a drop in the price, will want to close their position by buying if the price falls further to this level. This allows them to limit the loss rather than risk the price going up again.

Market greed

Traders who have previously taken their profits at the resistance level can identify the birth of a new trend and decide to re-enter the market. And they'll want to do it as close to their exit price as possible.

Both of these examples lead to increased buying pressure on the market and push prices higher. Once the new support level is established, there will also be a new level at which buyers will want to take their profits and sell. This creates a new level of resistance, progressively leading to an increase in support and resistance levels.

Chapter 13 - The Life of a Cryptocurrency Trader

When we decided to write this book, we wanted to provide a complete guide that not only taught people how to trade, but that gave them a true and reasonable perspective of what being a cryptocurrency trader really means.

This is why we have decided to ask Alvin Williams, a profitable crypto trader to tell us how he structures his day for maximum results. In the next few pages you are going to read his exact words. We would like to thank Alvin for sharing his expertise with us.

Alvin Williams tells us his trading lifestyle

Being a cryptocurrency trader today is in some respects 'easier' than when I started over 6 years ago, given that internet connections and trading platforms are much more advanced. Trading for a living, however, does not only concern our technical training and the ability to read and evaluate a certain situation on the cryptocurrency markets. It involves our emotional and experiential sphere as well. The trader's work is very fascinating because you are completely free. In fact you don't have set hours, employees or collaborators, a boss to be accountable to, suppliers or customers to manage. Therefore, it is not considered a classic work activity even if, on the inside, it has all the dynamics of a classic entrepreneurial activity. In fact, it is essential for professional trading to have a business plan to follow, a daily routine of actions to be performed, set times to follow the favorite cryptocurrencies and manage our work as a trader also from an administrative and financial point of view. As you can understand, all of these things are very close to what an entrepreneur does to grow his company.

What does a professional trader do?

Whoever does online trading buys and sells cryptocurrencies with the aim of making a profit. Traders can choose various types of assets on which to operate such as currencies (forex), bonds (bonds), equities (stocks), stock indices (indexes), commodities (commodities), cryptocurrencies. Let's say a trader tries to speculate on the price of an asset, then tries to make a profit from both rising and falling markets. Any type of trading or operational strategy carries risks. One of my dearest sayings is 'no losses, no gains', so you must think that to earn with trading you must have the ability to deal with expensive transactions (or accept the loss) to make a profit. The cryptocurrency markets are a beautiful place where those who know themselves and their method well can make a difference. However, those who do not know themselves well may not be able to turn trading into a profitable business.

There are many ways to trade, we can divide them into 4 main styles.

- **Position trading.** Infrequent trading activity, 4/5 positions per year, maintaining extremely long positions for months or years.
- **Swing trading.** More frequent but not excessive trading activity, 5/10 operations per month, maintenance of positions from one day to a few weeks at most.
- **Day trading.** Frequent activity, a few transactions are made every day, positions are maintained throughout the day and are not maintained overnight.
- **Scalping.** Very frequent trading activity, you can do even over 100 operations per day, maintaining the position for seconds or minutes.

Personally my favorite trading style is Swing Trading.

Life as a trader part 1: morning

In the morning my alarm goes off around 6:45 am. Immediately I take a shower and, after getting dressed, I prepare a rich breakfast for me and my family (I have two kids). For me, the daily diet is very important, to keep me fit both physically and mentally. In the morning, my breakfast is made up of all the macronutrients: proteins, carbohydrates and fats. Soon after I take the kids to school and by about 8:10 am I am at my office. Starting with a coffee is a must and immediately afterwards I go to the monitors and open

Binance and Coinbase to observe the markets in my main watchlist. I immediately look at those that I had marked the night before: my approach to trading is 'end of day trading' so every evening I write to myself the potential opportunities to follow the next day. At 9:00 am I connect to the virtual trading room that I created several years ago, where various traders subscribing to my operational service connect and with whom we analyze some situations and discuss the trading possibilities. At 10:30 I have a snack, while around 11:00 I do some form of physical activity. Physical activity in general is a cure-all for me and cannot be missed. At least 3 times a week I try to carve out this space. At 1:00pm I go to pick up my daughters from school and then go to eat something light.

Life as a trader part 2: early afternoon

After lunch, I go back to the office where I observe what happened in the morning. Subsequently, based on the day, I can do coaching sessions for some traders who want to learn my method or check emails or dedicate myself to the contents of my youtube channel or webinars, always things related to trading and my approach. Obviously, doing a scheduled trading on the daily / weekly chart I am not always in front of the monitor to observe every single price movement. On the contrary, for me the saying 'set and forget' is a philosophy to follow from day to day to remain calm and face markets with serenity and without 'distorted' emotions that can lead to worsening their results.

Life as a trader part 3: closing the markets

The cryptocurrency market does not have a real closure since it is open 24 hours a day, but it can still be seen that, based on the closure of the US stock markets, liquidity and exchanges drop significantly at that time. At that moment I always try to do an analysis of the closing of the day which, in some cases, can lead me to operate the next day. As mentioned, my approach is 'end of day trading' and therefore it is essential to operate on the basis of price action that happens at the end of the day.

Life as a trader part 4: trading on the weekend

For me the weekend is very important. The weekend becomes the main time for planning the next week's operations. I see everything without important movements that can disturb my view. At that moment I analyze the important levels of supply and demand and study the structure of the cryptocurrencies I follow the most. I note the main things that I will have to follow, with discipline, during the following week. According to my method, the weekend is the basis of all my operational trading.

Life as a trader part 5: my 7 tips

- Understand the trading style you want to use and therefore what trading method to follow. As you should know by now, swing trading is much different from day trading and vice versa.

- Decide the capital of your 'trading company'. Like any business you have to plan how much money you are willing to use for training.

- Create a 'business plan'. This involves markets on which to concentrate the most, operational time frames, types of signals to be used to enter and exit the market, percentage of risk on the single trade, maximum number of simultaneous operations, analysis / trading hours, operations management.

- Keep a trading diary. Write down all the trades made, their results, and possible notes. This serves to review what you have done. The diary is often very underestimated, but it is of great importance in the professional growth of the trader.

- Following a path of personal growth. Studying yourself, and learning how your brain and emotions work is certainly helpful in becoming a full-fledged trader.

- Staying in good physical shape, eating healthy without excess and leading a life that has a routine helps to improve concentration and perform better.

- Always stay humble. Even if you can earn a lot of money with trading, you should never change based on the money running in your pockets. Money comes and goes. On the contrary, time goes and doesn't come back so try to think of trading as a job that can help you improve your quality of life.

We would like to thank Alvin Williams once again for his help in the writing of this book. His expertise is truly valuable and we are honored to have him contribute to the realization of this cryptocurrency trading guide.

Chapter 14 - Bitcoin Options

The term "option" indicates a type of derivative contract that offers the owner the possibility (not the obligation) to buy or sell an asset at a certain price (strike price) in a predetermined period of time (the expiration date).

Although the term "derivative contract" usually evokes the idea of complex financial instruments created in the Wall Street laboratory, in ancient Greece, contracts similar to options were used to speculate on olive harvesting, and can be found in different cultures, as witnessed by the Japanese “Dojima Rice Exchange”, dating back to the 17th century. Today, options contribute to a global derivatives market with an estimated value of over $ 500 billion. So why are options such a consolidated and important part of finance, and what does the arrival of options on Bitcoin (BTC) mean for the crypto sector?

On an individual level, options allow market participants to generate income, place speculative bets and hedge their positions, especially in volatile market conditions. In an option contract, there is a seller (also called the writer) of the option and a buyer. The buyer pays a premium for the option contract, determined by factors that include moneyness (the current price of the asset vs. the strike price), the time left to expiration and the implied volatility; the writer takes this premium as income.

When applied to Bitcoin, this tool offers enormous benefits to many participants in the ecosystem. Long-term holders and miners can effectively hedge their positions and generate income by selling options, and speculators can limit downside risks and gain upside exposure for a fraction of the cost.

Looking at it as a whole, options have also proved crucial to the health of the market. According to a famous empirical analysis carried out by the Journal of Finance, options lead to "a reduction in spread and increases in quoted depth, trading volume, trading frequency and transaction size" and, overall, the results suggest that "options improve the market quality of the underlying securities." In other words, Bitcoin options can benefit the entire ecosystem, whether they are used by a specific individual or not.

Option contracts take two forms: call and put options. Call options give the buyer the opportunity to buy an underlying asset at a certain strike price, while put options give the buyer the opportunity to sell an underlying asset at a certain strike price.

Calls and puts offer writers and buyers the basic tools to speculate and / or hedge their portfolios. At the most basic level, the buyer of a call earns when the price of the underlying asset is greater than the strike price, and the buyer of a put earns when the underlying price is less than the strike price. But let's take a deeper look at how each contract works for each market operator.

The Long Call -- POV: Buy a call option. Sentiment: Bullish

A trader who buys a call option is convinced that the price of the underlying asset will increase. Even if traders could simply buy the asset directly, by doing so they would have direct exposure to a price risk up to its full value - particularly risky with a volatile asset class. However, when you buy a call, the risk is limited to the premium paid to purchase the option. On the other hand, the potential profit is determined by the difference between the spot price and the strike price, subtracting the premium. For example, if the strike price is $100 and the premium paid is $10, then a spot price of $120 will result in a profit of $10.

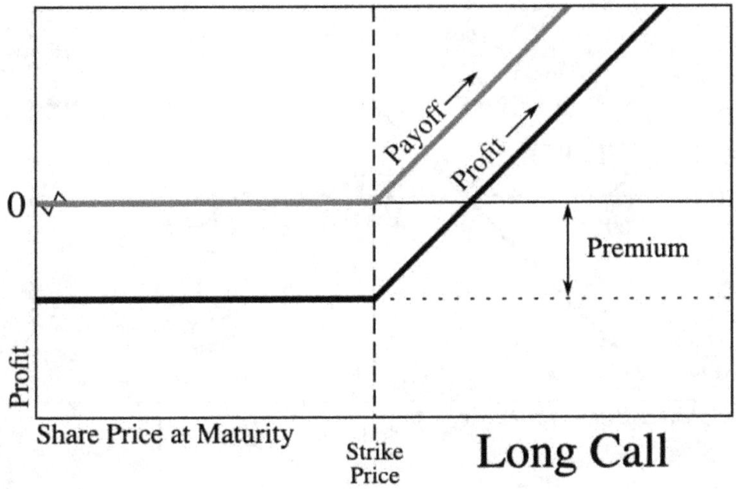

The Short Put -- POV: Selling a put option. Sentiment: Bullish

Another possibility for traders who are convinced that the price of an asset will increase is to sell a put option. When they sell a put option, traders agree to buy the underlying asset at the strike price if the buyers decide to exercise their right to sell. If the spot price of the asset is greater than the strike price, the buyers will decide not to sell, and the option writer will gain from the premium.

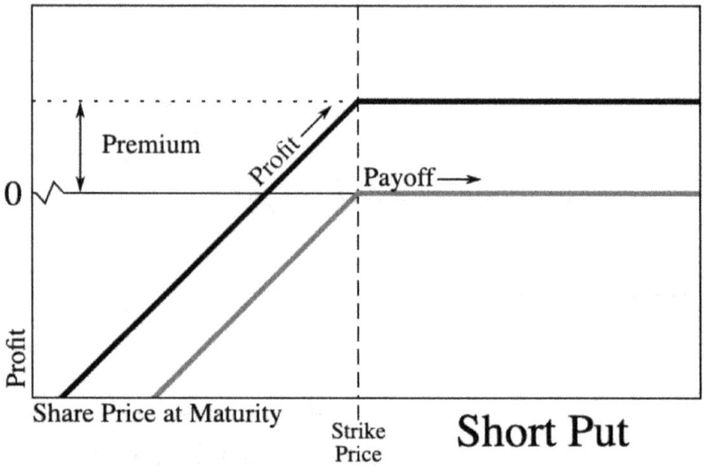

The Long Put -- POV: Buying a put option. Sentiment: Ribassist

If traders are bearish on the cryptocurrency in question, they can choose to buy a put option, which gives the right to sell at the strike price, instead of opening a short on the cryptocurrency. As with the Long Call described above, this limits the risk of loss to the premium paid for the option. When they buy a put option, traders earn if the spot price is below the strike price by more than the premium paid. For example, if the strike price is $100, and the premium paid is $10, then a spot price of $90 will remain even, and a lower price will yield a profit.

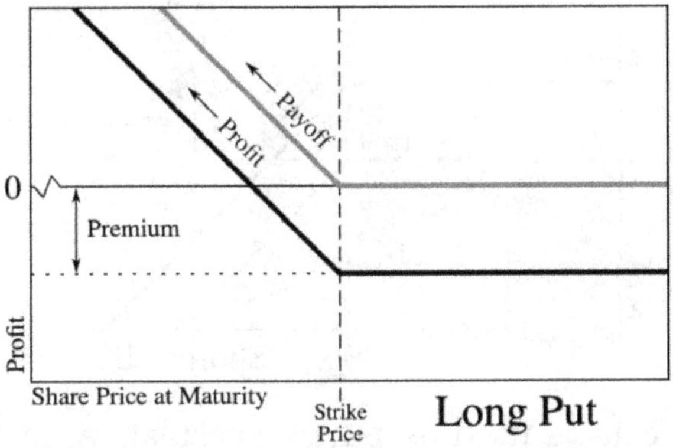

The Short Call -- POV: Selling a call option, Sentiment: Bearish

The other possibility for traders who expect a price drop is to sell a call option. In this case, the traders agree to sell the underlying asset at the strike price if the buyers exercise the right to purchase. As with the Short Put described above, this strategy aims to collect the premium on the option, when the buyers decide not to exercise the option. This occurs when the spot price is lower than the strike price. If the spot price is higher than the strike price, the writer of the call will have to sell the asset at a discounted price.

This strategy is commonly used as part of a covered call strategy, which is explained below.

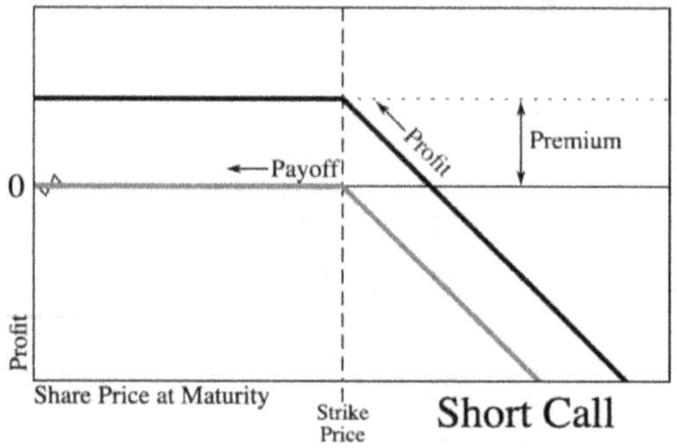

While options can be used as purely speculative investments, the most successful asset managers use them as a way to effectively mitigate risk and maximize potential gains. By combining the four basic trades using options (listed above) with the two basic trades (long and short), investors can create a number of more sophisticated strategies to optimize their portfolios.

The real power of options is not in their isolated use, but when they act as part of a broader strategy. When used in combination, they can model investor exposure to obtain a very specific risk profile, limit losses, generate income and achieve more predictable returns.

Covered Call

As mentioned above, one of the most popular options strategies is the Covered Call. In this strategy, investors have exposure to an asset and are optimistic over the long term, but do not expect a significant price increase in the short term. To still allow the asset to generate a return, traders sell a call option on the asset, receiving a profit in the form of a premium. This strategy is likely widespread, as we have already seen Bitcoin miners use futures contracts to hedge their positions. Now, miners can sell a $300 call option with a strike price of $10,000, to earn with the guarantee of a profit even in the event of a price increase.

Protective Put

A similar strategy for hedging a long-term investment is a simple Protective Put. Unlike the covered call, which limits the positive side of an investment if the call option is exercised and the asset sold, a protective put is intended to limit the negative side and at the same time preserve the positive one. In this case, traders buy a put option on a long-term investment as a hedge against potential losses, with a limit on the positive side equal only to the put premium. If investors have increased exposure during this recent downtrend with expectations of a surge, they may want to buy a $200 protective put with a strike price of $6,500, limiting the downside.

Put-Call Parity principle

Above all in these early stages of the market for Bitcoin options, arbitrage opportunities are also likely, according to the Put-Call Parity principle. This principle states that the difference between a call option and a put option with the same maturity and the same strike price is equivalent to the difference between the current spot price and the strike price, discounted at current values.

Covered calls and protective puts are just the beginning of a long series of strategies involving options. There are collar, straddle, strangle, butterfly and more. They can be broken down by market sentiment - bullish, bearish or neutral - and expected volatility.

$$C - P = S - K * D$$

Where C = value of the call option, P = value of the put option, S = spot price, K = strike price and D = discount factor.

When this equation is not valid, there is an arbitrage opportunity that traders can take advantage of - especially in the initial period of these options markets.

The price of the options (known as the premium) is determined by the market and is based on intrinsic and extrinsic value factors. The intrinsic value is the difference between the spot price of the underlying asset and the strike price but only in reference to a positive value for the option holder. When an option is not advantageous for the buyer, it is said to have zero intrinsic value and only extrinsic value, such as time value, strike price and volatility.

While several factors and highly complex valuation models are applied to calculate the value of various options, some of the most basic are quite simple. When an option is "in-the-money", i.e. the holders of the option will benefit from exercising their option, then the option has intrinsic value. An in-the-money option is easier to evaluate, as the intrinsic value is fixed, and the extrinsic value is a function of the risk associated with time value and volatility.

An out-of-the-money option, on the other hand, has no intrinsic value, so its price depends entirely on these extrinsic value factors. The premium, the option price, is equivalent to a commission that the option writer collects against the risk of selling. It should come as no surprise, then, that a volatile asset like Bitcoin presents such expensive rewards.

Over the past year, new trading platforms and options exchanges have emerged along with greater regulatory clarity. As already mentioned, options are critical to the health of an asset's market and to managing an individual's position in that market. These tools are also essential for attracting larger and more sophisticated investors and institutions.

Several platforms globally are growing to meet traders' demand for options, and even the CFTC seems to be on their side, considering the regulatory approval granted to LedgerX, Bakkt and CME Group.

We currently have a number of popular platforms dedicated to Bitcoin options trading, including Deribit, LedgerX, Quedex, Bakkt and most recently Binance. Each has its own set of pros and cons and should be evaluated according to the specific needs of the trader. Overall, we continue to see advances and developments in crypto financial infrastructure, and traders who manage to use these tools effectively can improve their returns.

Chapter 15 - Trading vs Investing

Is it better to trade or to buy and hold? Let's start from the common elements and continue analyzing in detail the differences between trading and investments to arrive at an answer. As far as the investment is concerned, it is obvious, but it is necessary to repeat it, we refer to the financial type of investment.

There are different forms of investment such as that in movable and tangible assets or that in more intangible assets and services. If you are here, and you will continue reading, you are investing in yourself, wise decision.

Both, investment and trading, require a small financial capital to be put into practice and both aim to increase this same capital. Again both aim at capital growth in order to make a profit or increase their own personal satisfaction. It should not be said that the investments also differ in the person who makes them.

Whether a private individual or an institutional body or a company. In this case the instruments are the same. What differentiates them are the purposes behind the investment choices. Very often when you have some savings you tend to set aside a small nest egg in order to reuse it or use it in emergency situations.

However, inflation tends to slowly erode this amount, whether large or small. Investments and trading make it possible to overcome the erosion of capital by inflation and make it increase, but there are differences, let's understand them better.

Conceptual differences

Investment and trading differ primarily in the following aspects.

- target
- time
- risk

Each of these three elements is different and this is also partly determined by the methodology of the two alternatives. Grasping these differences and being clear immediately about these elements automatically leads us to make the best choice for the use of our money. The investment fits very well for an asset protection goal while trading aims at a much more substantial increase.

Consequently, those who usually have smaller capital and need or want higher increases are traded. Investment, on the other hand, is well suited to those with huge wealth that are not interested in higher increases than not losing and protecting what they own.

Consequently, in trading, time refers to short-term and medium-term periods while investments love and bear fruit in the long term or even in the very long term. Think of pension funds or some American mutual funds that have a duration of twenty or forty years.

Because of the different objective and time, the risk is also different. In trading the risk is very high, you can lose even 30-40% of your investment and in the worst case and in those who trade in the wrong way you can lose all the money.

It is a concrete possibility and if you are a beginner, do not risk unnecessarily. In the investment, the risk profile given the longer time horizons and the purpose of protection rather than revaluation lead this component to be more contained.

Considering also the large capital that can be used and diversified, it makes the investment less risky. So investing the risk profile can be 5-15% per annum, if it were higher we had serious problems and making mistakes. By definition, trading is risky but you can manage this component by following specific rules that lower and shape the risk profile.

The risk profile can thus be raised or lowered in both by implementing more prudent activities in both trading and investment. It also follows that by implementing less attentive or less aware and informed behaviors, the risk and the possibility of loss increase significantly for both.

An example?

If we go to invest in a restricted capital fund for two years, but in a year we already know that we will have to buy a house, the investment becomes useless or even risky.

It is useless to lose the money for the opening commissions and then for the early release of the money and risky because it is possible that that money is not available for the fixed term. For this reason, before deciding whether it is better to trade or invest, you need to ask yourself a series of questions or ask your financial advisor who follows us.

Strategic differences

As we have seen trading is based on a series of “Buy and Sell” strategies, you buy and sell either on the same day or in the following days following specific strategies. On the contrary, the investment involves the purchase and possession for a longer term of the most suitable product.

The difference is a lot in the strategy and risk profile that you decide to run, from the personal skill and the uncontrollable trend of the markets. It is possible to obtain higher returns by taking much higher risks and however putting the entire capital at risk.

In investing, the returns are 5-15% per year, it may seem low but for those who invest it is completely acceptable given the greater capital and the compromise of having lower profits in exchange for the safety and constancy of the capital.

Here, too, the return as for trading can fluctuate depending on market trends and the instruments chosen. We then come to the last category of differences to understand whether it is better to trade or invest.

Methodological and operational differences

Substantial differences between trading and investing are above all at the level of technique. By technique we mean precisely the tools, methodology and approach employed.

It seems a bit obvious but it is like the difference between engineer and architect, both guarantee and make possible the construction of buildings. However, both make use of different tools, elements, programs, strategies that are only partially compatible and integrable. To make their choices, investors make use of fundamental analysis techniques while trading makes its decisions and sets strategies on technical analysis.

Since this is a book about trading, we can only recommend you to put a percentage of your net worth into this activity. However, we want to point out that investing is also a viable option to increase your capital on a regular basis.

Chapter 16 - Developing a Strong Mind

We would like to dedicate the last chapter of this book to a very important topic that most cryptocurrency traders often underestimate. In fact, even if you are incredibly good at identifying trends and managing your money, you will not go too far if you are not able to control your emotions and have a strong mind. In the following pages you are going to find some useful tips and tricks to stay strong and develop mental resilience even when things are not going too well.

Would you like to be able to face the ups and downs of trading with strength? Becoming mentally and emotionally strong is not something that happens overnight. If you are able to consider every little challenge that life presents to you as an opportunity to become stronger, you will begin to develop greater wisdom and mental clarity, which you can test when you find yourself facing real difficulties in your trading.

Understand what it means to be emotionally resilient

Being emotionally and mentally strong, or resilient, means knowing how to adapt to trading situations that present stress, trauma, adversity or tragic events. Resilience is not a quality that is acquired at the start of your trading career, it is a process that can be developed and learned by anyone.

Being emotionally strong does not mean never having to feel pain or suffering. On the contrary, resilience often develops when you are faced with an extremely painful situation. Being emotionally strong means learning to get up after a fall.

To become resilient you will need to commit to developing some specific skills. For example, you will need to learn to set and achieve goals, be more confident, develop a more positive outlook on yourself, manage intense impulses and emotions, and improve your problem-solving skills.

Learn the topic of "emotion regulation"

If you want to become mentally and emotionally strong, it is equally important to learn how to manage your emotions. Sometimes trading will present you with negative situations, it is inevitable. However, even then, you will always have the possibility to decide how to react. We are not talking about an innate gift, anyone can learn to manage their emotions in a constructive way.

Specifically identify the areas you want to change

Before you can develop greater mental and emotional strength, it is necessary to take an inventory of your current qualities and shortcomings to determine what is good to change in your trading. List as many of your strengths and weaknesses as possible on a piece of paper. Once you have completed the list, think about how you can turn each lack into a goal to be achieved.

For example, you may have written as one of your weaknesses that you have difficulty managing your positions. If you want to commit to improving in this area, you can decide that your goal is to study money management more carefully.

Recognize your strengths

In addition to identifying the aspects of yourself that you want to change, it's important to take the time to celebrate your qualities. Review the list of your positive qualities and congratulate yourself on each of them. From time to time, patting yourself on the back will help you stay focused on your positive qualities and become mentally and emotionally stronger.

Evaluate your past trades

The reasons why you may feel mentally and emotionally weak may be related to some past events. Whether it is a trade that occurred a few months ago or in the last session, your mental and emotional strength may still be affected. Research has found that traders who have been destroyed by the market are more prone to developing emotional and mental disorders that can lead them to abuse drugs or attempt suicide.

Try to determine if any negative trades may have contributed to your current mental and emotional state. Evaluate how and why they influenced your present.

Record your thoughts and feelings in a journal

Keeping a journal can help you recognize the origins of your weaknesses and is a great way to relieve stress effectively. Choose a quiet place and schedule to go there every day for 20 minutes to write in your journal. You can start by describing how you feel or what your thoughts are, or you can use the "prompting" technique to help initiate your responses. In this case, you can ask yourself questions to start the conversation with yourself.

Consider seeing a therapist

Sometimes, without professional help, it may not be easy to understand why you are having trouble and determine the best way to manage your feelings. A mental health professional can help you better understand your emotions and overcome them.

Note that your mental and emotional frailty may result from an underlying condition that needs to be treated. Talking to a therapist can help you better understand the dynamics of your mind and allow you to make the best decisions.

Stay away from vices that disturb your mental well-being

If you are endangering your mental health by drinking, using drugs, lying, stealing, etc. you are preventing yourself from becoming emotionally and mentally stronger. Start letting go of these bad habits or, at the very least, do what you can to limit them, to prevent them from taking control of your behaviors and emotions. If you have any addiction, ask for help.

Take care of yourself

Exercise, eat healthily, get enough sleep, and learn to relieve stress to help develop your mental and emotional strength. When you take good care of yourself, you send an important signal to your brain. Make sure you have plenty of time to meet your primary needs for exercise, nutrition, sleep and relaxation.

Empower your mind

Challenge it to constantly learn new things. As your trading knowledge increases, you will become mentally stronger and wiser. Don't allow yourself to get stuck in monotony, neither mental or physical. Try to always keep yourself curious, informed and aware. Read trading books and magazines, watch quality trading movies, go to concerts or the theater, attend a ballet and be interested in some form of art. In other words, commit yourself to self mastery.

Develop your spiritual side

Many people gain strength by paying attention to their spiritual side. Connecting with a higher entity, whatever it is, can instill strength and value in the spirit. Research has shown that spirituality and prayer can relieve stress and reduce the time it takes to recover from illness. Spirituality can take many forms and it is important to find the one that suits you best. There is no "correct" way to be spiritual.

Set reasonable trading goals and accomplish them

You can train your mental strength by setting meaningful goals and striving to achieve them gradually. Walking the path that will lead you to the goal requires commitment, the ability to overcome boredom or pain and a good dose of determination, necessary to not give up until the final goal is reached. There are no shortcuts, just practice will make your job easier.

If you have a very ambitious and seemingly unattainable goal, break it down into multiple sub-goals that are more easily achievable.

Once you commit to a goal, you have to decide that even if you take a misstep, you won't stop trying. In this way, you will also learn to see failure as an opportunity to learn something new.

Learn to resist negativity

Negativity can enter our lives in many different ways. For example from ourselves, in the form of an internal dialogue or negative thoughts, or from the outside, through opinions or offenses pronounced by others. While it is impossible to completely remove it from your life, there are many ways to learn how to deal with negativity.

While trying to minimize contact with negative or toxic people, sometimes you may not be able to completely eliminate them from your life. The people in question could be members of your family, colleagues or acquaintances with whom you need to interact. Instead of letting their negativity permeate you, you can learn not to get involved and set boundaries between you and those people.

Become mentally and emotionally strong through positive internal dialogue

Repeating positive affirmations on a daily basis can help you develop your mental and emotional strength. Take some time each day to look in the mirror and say self-encouraging phrases. You can choose to praise yourself for a quality you already possess or focus on an aspect you would like to develop. Here are some examples of positive affirmations:

"I'm working hard to get emotionally stronger and stronger."

"I'm learning to manage stress better and be kinder to myself."

"I know that by taking small daily steps towards my trading goal, I will feel emotionally and mentally stronger."

These sentences are extremely powerful, do not underestimate them.

Learn to stay calm when under pressure

When trading seems to escalate and you know you can lose your temper, instead of reacting impulsively try to remain calm to have more time to evaluate your options and find out which is the wisest choice to make.

Mentally counting to 10 might seem trivial, but it really works. Before you react emotionally to an event, stop, take a deep breath, and think carefully.

Let go of small things

By showing yourself overly sensitive to the inevitable setbacks and daily squabbles of trading, you will end up dedicating a good part of your time and energy to them every day. When you dwell on minor issues, turning them into real problems because of your attention, you not only increase your stress levels, but you also increase your risk of mortality. Learning to take a more constructive attitude, which allows you to overlook small things, will help you keep under control the levels of cortisol, the stress hormone, protecting you from any health disorders such as hypertension, heart disease, immune system and high cholesterol.

Instead of stressing yourself, get into the healthy habit of pausing to think about what is bothering you, then try to calm down and make the healthiest and most productive decision possible.

Keep your perfectionism in check

Being a perfectionist can mean having too high - and often unrealistic - expectations about yourself and others, sometimes forgetting that many of the situations we experience every day are beyond your control.

Try a visualization exercise to let go of the stress of small daily annoyances. Pick up a rock and imagine that it contains the source of your discomfort. Focus on that negative thing and clench your fist hard. Then, when you feel ready, throw the rock away. As you do this, imagine throwing away all the negative feelings associated with that stone as well.

Change perspective

If you tend to get trapped in your problems and worries, find ways to gain a different perspective on your trading. Anyone from time to time takes a dead end, but those who are mentally and emotionally strong are able to change course and find another way to reach the goal.

Be positive

Mentally and emotionally strong people tend to complain very rarely. While having to face the same challenges as anyone else, they are able to manage and put them in the right context. Being positive about what's good in your life, and the many possibilities that the future holds, will help you develop greater mental and emotional strength. It is useful for dealing with difficult trading situations. Studies have shown that a positive mental attitude can also benefit physical health.

Be honest with yourself

The ability to face reality is one of the hallmarks of a mentally and emotionally strong person. If you want to overcome an obstacle, you have to approach it directly. By lying to yourself about what is really going on you will end up hurting yourself.

If you have a tendency to run away from reality, try to recognize and overcome this bad habit.

Be honest with yourself about your weaknesses

Think before you act. When you are faced with a difficult situation, take your time to reflect before reacting or making a decision. This will give you the opportunity to regain control of your emotions and correctly weigh the options at your disposal.

If possible, take the time to evaluate the context by writing down your feelings. Do your best to try to identify at least one positive side, no matter how small it seems. Being able to change your perspective for a few moments could prove to be of great help. Remember to count to at least 10 before you say anything.

Determine what is the right thing to do and then do it

Let yourself be guided by your conscience. Research has shown that people who base their decisions primarily on instinct tend to feel more satisfied than those who study each choice down to the smallest detail. Sometimes the solution will be very clear, but on other occasions it may be very difficult to understand what is the right thing to do. Don't let the situation get worse and get out of hand - make a decision and stick with it.

Seek advice from people you trust. Asking the opinion of others when you are not sure what to do is completely acceptable. The important thing is not to be swayed into doing the wrong thing.

Think about what one of the people you admire would do. How would they act in your place? Last but not least, you must take responsibility for your actions. Make the best decision possible, making sure it doesn't generate regret.

Reflect on your experiences

After dealing with a complicated trade, evaluate what happened, the way you handled the circumstances and the result you achieved. Can you be proud of your behavior? Is there anything you could have done differently? Try to learn the most from every trade you have done. Wisdom only develops through this type of practice. Instead of simply trying to forget and move on, examine what happened - so the next time you have to make a decision, you know what to do.

Unfortunately, trades do not always go as smoothly as we hope and we are not always able to obtain the desired results; it is a universal truth, which is valid for everyone, even for those who apparently have a perfect trading strategy. Realizing the reality of this affirmation will allow you to be much more calm and collected when facing a difficult situation.

Conclusion

Congratulations on making it to the end of this book, we hope you found some useful insights to take your cryptocurrency trading skills to the next level. As you should know by now, the world of cryptocurrency is extremely complicated and there is a new "opportunity" every way you look. However, our experience tells us that only by taking things seriously and having a proper plan you can develop your trading skills to the point that you can trade for a living.

Our final advice is to stay away from the shining objects that the world of cryptocurrencies offers you every day. Choose a cryptocurrency you want to master and study it in depth. After you have a sufficient knowledge on what you are talking about, apply the fundamental and technical analysis strategies we have discussed in this book. Analyze your results, improve your money management skills and become the master of your emotions.

As you can see, there are no shortcuts you can take. Easy money does not exist. What exists is the possibility to start from zero and work your way up to become a professional trader. The journey might be difficult, but it is certainly worth it.

To your success!

Bitcoin Revolution

The Ultimate Bitcoin and Blockchain Guide to Master the World of Cryptocurrency and Take Advantage of the 2021 Bull Run!

Additionally, the information in the following pages is intended only for informational purposes and should thus be thought of as universal. As befitting its nature, it is presented without assurance regarding its prolonged validity or interim quality. Trademarks that are mentioned are done without written consent and can in no way be considered an endorsement from the trademark holder.

Table of Contents

Introduction

Bitcoin has taken the world by storm once again when it crossed $20,000 per BTC in December of last year. After more than 2 years of bear market, the most famous cryptocurrency surpassed its previous all time high.
A lot of people are now trying to improvise themselves as professional investors and are losing a lot of money, only helping those who actually know what they are doing accumulate an incredible amount of wealth that will lead to generational fortunes.

To join the club of the few investors that actually make it, you need the right strategies and the right mindset. Notice how we did not include a large initial capital. In fact, while having more money to trade with means having more fire power, it is not necessary to have thousands of dollars to accumulate Bitcoin and build wealth.

In fact, when we started investing in Bitcoin we only had a few hundreds to put into the market, but that sum yielded us thousands and thousands of dollars over the span of a few years.

In this book you are going to discover all the strategies that have allowed us to take investing skills to the next level and everything that helped us understand Bitcoin. If you diligently apply our advice, we are sure you are going to see amazing results in a relative short period of time, since this bull run is offering an amazing number of opportunities.

Please, stay away from all the shiny objects of the cryptocurrency world. Just focus on Bitcoin, study it deeply and then milk it like a cash cow!

To your success!

Charles Swing and *Masaru Nakamoto*

Chapter 1 - What is Bitcoin?

Bitcoin (฿, BTC, XBT) is a cryptocurrency otherwise called cryptographic currency. In the case of the unitary denomination, it is written "bitcoin" and, in the case of the peer-to-peer payment system, it is written "Bitcoin". The idea was first presented in November 2008 by one person, or a group of people, under the pseudonym Satoshi Nakamoto. The source code for the implementation of Bitcoin was released in 2009.

The G20 considers Bitcoin to be a “crypto-asset”. The term “crypto-asset” refers to “virtual assets stored on an electronic wallet allowing a community of users accepting them in payment to carry out transactions without having to resort to legal tender”.

Operation

To create and manage bitcoins, Bitcoin relies on software. In this software, bitcoins are created according to a protocol that pays the agents (called “miners”) who have processed transactions. These agents use their computing power to verify, secure and record the transactions in a virtual ledger called the blockchain. The word blockchain comes from the fact that the basic entity of Bitcoin is called a block, and that the blocks are then connected in a chain.

For each new block accepted, the verification-security-recording activity, called mining, is remunerated by newly created bitcoins and by the costs of the transactions processed. As a currency or a commodity, bitcoin can be exchanged for other currencies or commodities, goods or services. The cryptocurrency exchange rate is set on specialized marketplaces and fluctuates according to the law of supply and demand.

It is possible to buy bitcoins online on specialized platforms, physical terminals or in exchange for any good or service with a person who already has them (the transaction can be done from smartphone to smartphone). The platforms also make it possible to follow in real time the evolution of the price of bitcoin compared to other currencies or cryptocurrencies.

Account unit

Bitcoin's unit of account is bitcoin. Its emission is limited to 20,999,999.977 units, each divisible to the eighth decimal place (called Satoshi or Sat). The official currency symbol was registered and accepted in 2015 with Unicode. The corresponding acronyms, used by the exchange platforms, are BTC and XBT. Among the unofficial symbols used are ฿ and Ƀ.

Decentralization

The system operates without a central authority or a single administrator. It is managed in a decentralized manner thanks to the consensus of all the nodes of the network. Bitcoin is the largest decentralized crypto currency, with a capitalization of over one trillion dollars as of April 5th, 2021 ($ 130 billion as of January 1st, 2020).

Means of payment

As a means of payment, bitcoin is accepted by a growing number of merchants, encouraged by transaction fees generally lower than the 2 to 3% charged by credit card organizations and independent of the amount of the financial transaction. However, in 2017 the fees increased dramatically over the course of a few months, from $0.2 in 2016 to $20 on certain days in December 2017, so that the Steam platform or Microsoft withdrew Bitcoin as a payment method, precisely because of too high transaction fees (Microsoft again authorized Bitcoin in January 2018).

In order to address the issue of excessively high transaction fees, the gradual rollout of various technology enhancements (Segwit, Lightning Network, batch transactions, Schnorr) throughout 2018 and 2019 allowed fees to drop to around $0.05 for non-urgent transactions, and even amounts less than $ 0.0001 for Lightning type transactions. Unlike credit cards, any charges are borne not by the seller but by the buyer, who chooses to pay them voluntarily. A bitcoin transaction is irrevocable and cannot be reversed. Despite a 500% growth in the number of merchants accepting bitcoin in 2014, the cryptocurrency is not very established in the retail trade, but continues to gain a foothold in trade.

Use

Between January 2009 and March 2010, using bitcoin was a hobby among crypto enthusiasts, and bitcoin had no real value. However, in April 2010, bitcoin started trading in an exchange for $0.003, and soon after, in May 2010, it was already worth $0.01. A few months later, in July 2010, 0.08 dollars were added to its value again. These numbers reflect the rapid rise in prices that this zero-value cryptocurrency has experienced at 10 cents.

Since its creation in 2009 and until the closure by the American authorities of Silk Road in 2013, bitcoin was used mainly as a medium of exchange by criminal networks for gambling, the purchase of illicit substances, or for hacked databases. The cryptocurrency has attracted the attention of financial authorities, legislative bodies in various countries, particularly the United States, and the mainstream media.

Nevertheless, in recent years, cryptocurrency has matured and a growing number of studies conclude that these illegal activities, although they still exist as in any payment system, only involve a minority share of cryptocurrency exchanges. The United States Senate also recognizes that bitcoin makes it possible to provide perfectly legitimate financial services.

Safe store of value

According to some of the experts, bitcoin would be a safe haven much more than a means of payment, even if unlike gold, Bitcoin can indeed be used for these two purposes. Conversely, other financial experts consider Bitcoin to be far too volatile to be a safe haven, but it has only existed since 2009 and its possible safe haven status will only be possible after a first period of intense volatility . As for the question of whether Bitcoin can reach the market value of gold (or even exceed it), this remains much debated. However, it should be noted that with its trillion dollars evaluation, Bitcoin is not too far from reaching the value of Silver, which is approximately 1.4 trillion dollars.

Chapter 2 - The History of Bitcoin

Bitcoin is an improvement on the concept of b-money, imagined by Wei Dai in 1999, and bitgold, described in 2005 by Nick Szabo. Bitcoin in particular solves the crucial problem of the trust model: servers considered serious vote with their computing power to determine the legitimate transaction chain. In b-money, the servers were supposed to pay a security deposit according to a not very explicit mechanism. The idea of using a computational proof chain was put forward in the bitgold project although Nick Szabo only proposed to use a majority of addresses to establish the legitimacy of a chain of transactions, which left the problem of controlling the number of addresses.

Satoshi Nakamoto claimed that he worked on bitcoin from 2007 to 2009. As early as 2008, he posted a document on a mailing list describing the digital currency. In February 2009, he published an announcement about his work on the P2P Foundation site. On January 3, 2009, the first block or genesis block was created. In February 2009, he distributed the first version of the Bitcoin software on the P2P Foundation site and to operate the network, he used his computer and thus generated the first bitcoins. Along with other developers, Nakamoto continued the implementation of the software and its Bitcoin-Qt version until 2010.

Developers and the bitcoin community gradually lost contact with him in the middle of 2010. On December 12, 2010, a final message was posted by Nakamoto on the main forum. Shortly before disappearing, Nakamoto designates Gavin Andresen as his successor by giving him access to the SourceForge bitcoin project and a copy of the alert key. The latter is a unique private cryptographic key allowing to mitigate the effects of a potential attack on the Bitcoin system, such as the discovery of a cryptographic flaw allowing to modify the transactions, or the take of control of more than 51% of the nodes in the network. During an alert, the operators of the nodes of the network can either warn their users or stop recording transactions.

On September 27, 2012, the Bitcoin Foundation was created. Important characters from the world of new technologies quickly supported the project, such as Wences Casares.

The identity of Satoshi Nakamoto

Several people claimed to be Satoshi Nakamoto, but none of them could prove it. There is no trace of his identity before the creation of Bitcoin. On his profile, Satoshi claimed to be a 40-year-old Japanese.

In March 2014, journalist Leah McGrath Goodman from Newsweek magazine announced that she had tracked down the inventor of Bitcoin who she said would be a 64-year-old Japanese-American whose birth name is "Satoshi Nakamoto", although he changed his name to "Dorian Prentice Satoshi Nakamoto" at the age of 23. He is believed to be a retired physicist living in California. This thesis was methodically dismantled a month later by linguists from Aston University in England who carried out an in-depth study of the linguistic correspondences between the written productions of the author of the Bitcoin white paper and several suspected personalities, notably Dorian Nakamoto.

In 2016, Craig Steven Wright, an Australian entrepreneur, claimed to be Satoshi Nakamoto. However, strong doubts remain.

Adoption

The history of Bitcoin adoption is quite remarkable, as it has been a long process of fake bans and unjustified threats to the cryptocurrency space. In the following pages we are going to track back the adoption process of Bitcoin, starting from 2012. Here are the main milestones of BTC adoption.

- On November 16th, 2012, WordPress started accepting bitcoins for its paid services.

- On November 28th, 2012, the remuneration of miners decreased for the first time, from 50 to 25 BTC. The bitcoin source code provides for a halving of the remuneration every two hundred and ten thousand blocks mined, or approximately every four years.

- On December 6th, 2012, a partnership between the startup Paymium (French exchange site) and the company Aqoba (payment institution) enabled Paymium to operate as a payment service provider, and therefore to keep accounts in euros and issue payment cards usable in euros and bitcoins. On February 14th, 2013, the Reddit community site set up a system to buy "Reddit Gold" with bitcoins.

- On February 16th, 2013, the online storage site Mega, successor to Megaupload, started accepting payments in bitcoin. On October 14th, 2013, the giant Baidu (Chinese equivalent of Google) started accepting bitcoin transactions for its Jiasule firewall service.

- On October 29th, 2013, the first automatic bitcoin cash dispenser-exchanger went into service in Vancouver. In September 2016, more than seven hundred and seventy of these automatic distributor-exchangers were installed worldwide, including four in France.

- On November 21st, 2013, the University of Nicosia announced that it accepted bitcoin and opened a master's degree in economics specializing in digital currencies. On November 22nd, 2013, Richard Branson announced that Virgin Galactic was going to accept bitcoins as a means of payment for its space tourism flights.

- On November 29th, 2013, Jiangsu Telecom (third largest Chinese operator), a subsidiary of China Telecom, started accepting bitcoins.

- On March 25th, 2014, the US tax authorities declared that bitcoin should not be considered as a currency, but as a commodity, whose transactions are subject to taxation on capital gains. This involves taking into account the exchange rate at which a bitcoin has been acquired and the one at which it is used in order to calculate the realized gain, which makes the legal use of bitcoin in the United States particularly difficult.

- On May 9th, 2014, the United States Election Commission accepted that election campaigns could be funded in bitcoins up to a limit of $100 per election cycle.

- On September 23rd, 2014, Paypal allowed certain North American digital goods merchants selected by partner bitcoin payment processors to accept payments in bitcoins, and thus very gradually opened up to bitcoin. As of October 16th, 2017, there were Bitcoin ATMs around the world.

- In December 2017, the French Minister of Public Accounts, Gérald Darmanin, reminded French taxpayers of the requirement to declare income, when it comes to capital gains realized during bitcoin transactions.

- In November 2018, the Ohio government announced that it was accepting Bitcoin tax payments. In January 2020, an investing.com study revealed that 9% of financial advisers already put part of their client's funds in bitcoin to protect them from monetary troubles.

Important moments

During the adoption phase there have been quite a few important moments that changed the course of Bitcoin's life. Here are the most important ones.

On August 15th, 2010, a block was generated containing a transaction creating 184,467,440,737 bitcoins for three different addresses. This flaw is linked to the fact that the code did not foresee the case of creating such large amounts of bitcoins. This problem was solved automatically by the bitcoin blockchain and these bitcoins no longer exist.

On March 12th, 2013, an incident occurred related to the non-backward compatibility of version 0.8.0: the chain split into several versions and some remained blocked for a few hours. After a few moments of panic, the system was able to correct itself, signaling the strength of the blockchain technology.

On April 11th, 2013, the value of bitcoin collapsed from $266 to $105 before stabilizing at $160 in less than six hours. On April 13th, the price reached $66. This massive drop occurred after a big bull run, where the price of Bitcoin rose six times in just a few weeks. For those that are already familiar with Bitcoin's price action, we are sure they are smiling just by thinking about such low prices.

On October 2nd, 2013, Ross Ulbricht was arrested. He was the alleged founder of Silk Road, which was shut down by the FBI and used only bitcoin for all of its transactions. More on that in a dedicated chapter.

On February 11th, 2014, the Bitcoin network was the victim of a massive and concerted attack launched on numerous exchange platforms, where quite a few bitcoins were stolen. This was just the preview of what was going to happen a few days later. In fact, on February 24th, 2014, the Mt. Gox trading platform suffered a record loss of 744,408 BTC, the equivalent of more than 44 billion dollars. The site was closed shortly after. A crisis management document has been drawn up and is publicly available on its website, we suggest you check it out because it is quite interesting (https://www.mtgox.com/). Due to this incident, bitcoin lost more than 38% of its value in the first quarter of 2014. On September 11th, 2015, Mark Karpelès, owner of the Mt. Gox platform was indicted in Japan for embezzlement. He is suspected of having embezzled 2.3 million dollars of bitcoin deposits.

In May 2016, the Gatecoin exchange site was hacked and had 250 bitcoins and 185,000 ether stolen. The hacker managed to bypass the online storage limits of the exchange platform's assets: while only 5% of the deposits are not cold stored, the hacker managed to empty these deposits while continuing to feed the address by transfer of cold storage assets from the exchange platform. After this event, almost every trading and exchanging platform decided to implement a new protection mechanism, in order to improve their safety.

On August 3rd, 2016, the Bitfinex exchange site reported the theft of 119,756 bitcoins on its exchange platform, which at the time counted for around $65 million.

On May 7th, 2019, hackers stole more than 7,000 Bitcoins from the Binance Cryptocurrency Exchange, worth over US $40 million. Binance CEO Zhao Changpeng said, “Hackers used a variety of techniques, including phishing, viruses and other attacks. They had the patience to wait and perform well orchestrated actions through multiple independent accounts at the most opportune moment”. It was this event that inspired Binance to improve its protection mechanism even further.

All incidents related to exchange platforms only affect people who do not themselves hold the private keys of their bitcoin wallet. Not your keys, not your bitcoins as they say. As you can see, every time the Bitcoin network has been attacked, new solutions were found to make sure the same issue would not happen in the future. In our opinion, this is one of the main strengths in this system. In fact, since it is developed by people, it can easily adapt to new hacking methods and attacks. It is pretty interesting to see the evolution of Bitcoin and if you want to actually invest in it safely, you need to know a bit of its history as well.

A common hacking technique

The technique known as the Trojan Horse makes it possible to change the address of the recipient of the cryptocurrency transaction. CryptoShuffler is one of the software using this technique. This rare technique has little effect because it suffices for the payment sender to visually check the first/last characters of the destination address to make sure that it is not being fooled.

Price evolution against the dollar

When it was created in February 2009, the cryptocurrency was initially traded only as an experiment by a few rare users and its value was zero. On October 12th, 2009, the first known bitcoin sale took place, where two users traded 5,050 bitcoins for $5.02 using a Paypal transfer, which equates to a price of around $0.001 per bitcoin.

In March 2010, Bitcoinmarket.com was the first bitcoin exchange platform to be opened, thus allowing continuous quotation of the price of bitcoin. It was the beginning of an era and every Bitcoin enthusiast should be thankful to this website for what it has done for the community.

On February 9th, 2011, bitcoin reached the valuation of one full dollar. On November 29th, 2013, the value of a bitcoin exceeded that of an ounce of gold, to nearly $1,250. Once again, for those that are familiar with today price action, these numbers do not seem so incredible. However, if you think about it, we are talking about a huge price development in just a couple of years. What other asset did over 1000% in just two years? The answer is very simple: no other asset managed to do it.

Bitcoin, mainly traded for yuan and dollars, can also be traded for euros on a dozen platforms. Until November 2013, Mt. Gox was the most important of these platforms in terms of transaction volume (~ 70%) and the practice had been taken to consider its price as representative of the market. As a result of the problems encountered, users turned away from it, causing the price of bitcoin to drop sharply on Mt. Gox, with prices observed on other platforms only slightly affected.

The price experienced a 400% increase between January and March 2013, before correcting itself severely on April 10th, following a failure of the Mt. Gox exchange site and probable panic sales. The price fell back to the level of the previous month, around $50. Between December 4th and 5th, 2013, following a warning from the People's Bank of China and the Bank of France, the price lost nearly 35% in 24 hours.

On February 19th, 2014, the price collapsed following the announcement of the disappearance of 850,000 bitcoins on Mt. Gox. On this exchange platform, bitcoin goes from $185, on February 18, to $73 24 hours later, while it remains close to $400 on other platforms. Mt.Gox declared bankruptcy on February 28, 2014. On May 1st, 2014, a group of investors by the name of Sunlot Holdings offered to buy the site for one symbolic bitcoin.

In 2016, after the Brexit announcement on June 24th, the value of bitcoin skyrocketed, gaining more than 9%, while all financial centers plunged for more than a week. This was probably the first time that the true strength of Bitcoin was shown to the world. In fact, BTC is an asset that does particularly well when there is turbulence in the world. We have seen this in 2020, where it rose by over 600% in just one year.

In 2017, Bitcoin topped out at around $19,000 and entered a long bear market of over 2 years. Those who accumulated during that time were brave enough to survive more than 700 days without seeing the asset climbing back to its all time high. However, in 2020, Bitcoin finally managed to break that level and skyrocketed. At the time of writing this book, one bitcoin is worth around $60,000.

Think about it, if you bought $10 worth of Bitcoin on February 9th, 2011, you would now have an equivalent of over $600,000. These kind of numbers really impress us.

Chapter 3 - The Idea behind Bitcoin

Bitcoin's theoretical roots lie in the Austrian school of economics and its critique of the current monetary system and interventions by governments and other entities, which this school of thought says exacerbates business cycles and massive inflation.

One of the topics that the Austrian School of Economics, led by Eugen von Böhm-Bawerk, Ludwig von Mises and Friedrich A. Hayek, focused on is the business cycle. In fact, according to the Austrian theory, business cycles are the consequence of inevitable monetary interventions in the market, whereby an excessive expansion of bank credit leads to an increase in the stock of bank credit in a fractional reserve system, which in turn leads to artificially low interest rates.

In this situation, entrepreneurs, guided by distorted interest rate signals, embark on over-ambitious investment projects that do not match the preferences of consumers at that time for intertemporal consumption (that is, i.e. their short-term decisions and future consumption). Sooner or later, this generalized imbalance can no longer last and leads to a recession, during which companies must liquidate failed investment projects and restructure their production structures according to the intertemporal preferences of consumers. As a result, many economists in Austrian schools are calling for the abandonment of this process by abolishing the fractional reserve banking system and reverting to a currency based on the gold standard, which cannot be easily manipulated by authorities.

A related area in which Austrian economists have been very active is monetary theory. Friedrich A. Hayek is one of the best known names in this field. He wrote some very influential publications, such as Denationalization of Money (1976), in which he postulated that governments should not have a monopoly on issuing money. On the contrary, he suggests that private banks should be allowed to issue non-interest bearing certificates, based on their own trademarks. These certificates (i.e. currencies) should be open to competition and would be traded at varying exchange rates. Any currency that can guarantee stable purchasing power would eliminate other less stable currencies from the market. The result of this process of competition and profit maximization would be a highly efficient monetary system in which only stable currencies would coexist.

The following ideas are generally shared by Bitcoin supporters.

- They see Bitcoin as a good starting point to end the monopoly of central banks in issuing money.

- They strongly criticize the current fractional reserve banking system, which allows banks to extend their credit supply beyond their actual reserves and, at the same time, allows depositors to withdraw their funds to their checking accounts at any time.

Specificity of Bitcoin

We must distinguish between bitcoin, cryptocurrency and on the other hand Bitcoin, the payment system in this currency. In these two aspects, Bitcoin differs from pre-existing systems on some important points.

First of all, unlike other monetary currencies, Bitcoin is not the embodiment of the authority of any state, bank, or business. The value of bitcoin is determined in a fully floating fashion by the economic use that is made of it and by the foreign exchange market. The rules organizing the monetary issue are determined solely by the free computer code of the Bitcoin software.

Furthermore, as a payment system, Bitcoin is distinguished by the fact that its operation does not require the use of a centralized infrastructure keeping accounts of the amounts held in order to ensure transactions. The role of guarantee and verification exists, but is assigned approximately every ten minutes to a computer of the network chosen at random according to its power.

Bitcoin is based on a cryptographic protocol whose main purpose is, on the one hand, to resolve the so-called double payment problem, which had hitherto prevented the emergence of such a type of currency, and, on the other hand, to "prohibit" the falsification of stakeholder identifiers and the value of bitcoin stock in electronic wallets identified by a given address.

Monetary principles behind Bitcoin

From a monetary point of view, bitcoin is distinguished from other currencies by the major fact that the monetary aggregate is not designed to adapt to the production of wealth.

The total amount and the emission rate of the units are entered explicitly in the computer code of the software, according to a mathematical rule of the geometric series type. Bitcoins are issued slowly and steadily, decreasingly, reaching a maximum amount of 21 million around the year 2140.

All fiat currencies experience inflation, from low to high depending on the policies of their central bank. Conversely, bitcoin currency is likely to end up experiencing deflation, as the maximum amount of bitcoins that can be created is set in the software in advance at 21 million. In addition to this, bitcoins lost by users will never be replaced. This is why the Bitcoin project is considered by the community of its creators as an original experiment in economic terms, constituting a kind of test of the monetary theses of the Austrian school of economics. In fact, Friedrich Hayek, Nobel laureate in economics, in 1976 called for the reestablishment of monetary free will in his book "For a true competition of currencies". The success or failure of Bitcoin is difficult to predict, but it is impossible to say it has not done well so far.

Scalability of the protocol

On July 14th, 2010, shortly after the launch of the Bitcoin system, Satoshi Nakamoto created a limit of 1MB for each newly created block every ten minutes on the bitcoin blockchain.

At that time, transactions were free because few in number, and developers had a legitimate concern that attackers could "spam" the transaction network, arbitrarily creating huge blocks and permanently inflating the size of the blockchain. This limit was intended to prevent this kind of attack until a better solution could be put in place. Satoshi Nakamoto had proposed a solution that would involve increasing the block size to certain block heights, effectively increasing the limit to a predetermined rate similar to how new bitcoins are issued.

The scalability of the Bitcoin system has been a constant source of debate in the community since the introduction of this block size limit. This 1 MB limit, initially thought to limit the number of transactions per second to seven, posed no problem at a time when the actual number of transactions hardly exceeded 2.3 transactions per second (2010). So, seven transactions per second was three times the volume of bitcoin's busiest day at that time, leaving developers years to find a better solution. In addition to this, the protocol provided for the introduction of transaction fees over time, which would make this type of attack more costly and ineffective.

Saturation of transaction integration capacity

From 2014, the success of the Bitcoin system led to a continuous rise in the number of transactions which eventually hit the 1MB limit in 2016. A developer, Gavin Andresen, initially proposed 20MB blocks, but the increase was deemed too aggressive by the community. Another proposal, BIP10191, offered to increase the block size by 40% per year from 8MB which led to the creation of a new cryptocurrency, different from bitcoin, called Bitcoin XT92.

Other proposals have been made like BIP10093 with a 2MB block which leads to the Bitcoin Classic cryptocurrency and more aggressive "emerging consensus" approaches that allow users to "vote" on the best block size at a time given through Bitcoin Unlimited.

Other members of the community preferred not to favor an increase in the block size, but to change the protocol itself so that more transactions are integrated in a block by reducing their size or increasing the creation frequency of new blocks.

When the number of transactions eventually reached the block size limit, the pool of pending transactions became full. The only way to get a given transaction into the blockchain faster for a user was to increase transaction fees, which reached nearly $5 at the end of 2016. This made Bitcoin uncompetitive against existing services like Western Union or Paypal on the strict basis of speed and cost.

The New York Agreement

The stalled debate on scalability weakened the Bitcoin Core system and led to the growing success of the vote in favor of the Bitcoin Unlimited movement, especially among miners, in large part due to frustration at the lack of upgrading solutions. The approach of the development team, called segwit (segregated witness), of not increasing the block size limit, but differently partitioning the digital signatures of transactions into "extension block", was not working to achieve sufficient consensus.

A compromise was found in an industry consensus in 2017 called Segwit2x97, which combined the segregated witness proposal with a block size increase to 2MB. This proposal was implemented on August 1st, 2017 for segregated witnesses and the block size increase came into effect in November 2017 at block 494,784. It was a major update to the Bitcoin system.

Nonetheless, the scalability debate was still heated and a breakaway group unilaterally increased the block size to 8MB while rejecting the Segwit proposal on August 1, 2017. This decision led to the emergence of a new cryptocurrency, called Bitcoin Cash.

Bitcoin XT (created in August 2015), Bitcoin Unlimited (created in January 2016), Bitcoin Classic (created in February 2016 before being discontinued in November 2017), Bitcoin Cash (created in August 2017) and Bitcoin Gold (created in October 2017) are alternative cryptocurrencies to Bitcoin (also called Bitcoin Core) that try to solve the problem of transaction fees.

Distribution of wealth

Bitcoins are concentrated in the hands of a few whales. The distribution of "wealth" is such that 2,100 addresses hold 40.2% of the total. However this kind of information is not very useful because some of these addresses are dead (keys lost when a unit of bitcoin was not worth 1 cent). Our opinion is that now that we are seeing institutions jumping on board, we will have much more concentration in terms of the number of bitcoins owned by whales. As the price rises, it will be more and more difficult for the average Joe to have ownership of one full bitcoin.

Chapter 4 - How Bitcoin Works

Bitcoin does not have an independent existence of the Bitcoin payment system which allows transactions to be made from one account to another, thanks to software called wallets, and the authority being ensured by software from verification called miners. The data of all transactions constitute a public ledger under private law called "blockchain" because of its structure, and an agent uses bitcoins by recording their transactions in the Bitcoin system's blockchain.

The Bitcoin system is computer-based. In other words, the Bitcoin system resides on the Internet. Downloading and installing the appropriate software allows you to become a Bitcoin user by interacting with hardware of your choice, including a smartphone or computer. To pay or be paid in bitcoin, the user must connect to the system. This connection offers two functions: the creation of any number of accounts, and the ease of carrying out transactions consisting of the transfer of bitcoins from an own account to the account of a third party.

The essential function of the Bitcoin system lies in the transactions which are subjected to a validity check by the competent computers and are irrevocably entered in a public register. This public ledger or blockchain can be viewed anywhere by anyone, as long as they have an internet connection. During the consultation no alteration is possible.

Bitcoin transaction mechanism

A Bitcoin transaction requires two fundamental steps.
First, dedicated network nodes (the “miners”) create a new block by grouping together recently completed transactions and adding a header to them containing the date and time, a checksum (“hash "), which will also serve as the unique identifier of the block, and the identifier of the previous block.

Secondly, after having checked the validity of all the transactions contained in this new block and their consistency with the transactions already recorded, each miner adds it to their local version of the register (or chain of blocks).
The public register is copied several times. The complete history of all transactions can then be read by viewing all nodes in the network that manage a copy of the blockchain. The copy can reveal possible differences between files, in the event of disagreement. In this case, any differences between these copies must be resolved by the software.

If you think about it, transactions consist of debiting certain accounts in order to credit others.

They are made up of inputs and outputs. Each output includes an amount and the public key of the credited address, or more generally a program (a script) making it possible to authorize or not the transfer of the amount of this output to another transaction. Each input designates an output from a previous transaction and has a program (script) that provides the data expected by the script appearing in that output. The sum of the values of the outputs must be less than or equal to the sum of the values of the inputs. The difference constitutes the miner's remuneration.

When creating a transaction, scripts for each entry are executed; first the script of the entry itself, then the script of the earlier exit that the entry refers to. The transaction is only committed if the result is "true" for all inputs.

These scripts are written in an internal language designed by Nakamoto. This language is intentionally minimalist and not Turing-complete in order to prevent the system from being able to engage in infinite loops. The use of scripts should allow the software to easily adapt to future developments and allow support for advanced features such as transactions involving multiple signatures or smart contracts.

Transactions made by a node are broadcast to its neighbors. These validate the transactions they receive and gradually consolidate them into a local pool before passing them on to their own neighbors. The valid transactions are thus broadcast step by step to all the nodes of the network, after a new check during each step.

Before permanently registering a transaction in the blockchain, the network performs several times a set of checks, including in particular that the outputs referenced by the inputs do exist and have not yet been used, that the author of the transaction is indeed the owner of the address credited in these outputs, and that the sum of the amounts appearing in the outputs of the transaction is much less than or equal to the sum of the amounts of the outputs referenced by the inputs. It is a bit complicated, but if you read this last sentence a couple of times you will get a better grasp of what actually happens during a transaction.

The effect of entering a transaction in the blockchain is to prohibit any future reference to the outputs designated by the inputs of this transaction, and therefore to prevent a double expenditure of the amount of these outputs, which would amount to creating from scratch bitcoins in an unauthorized manner. The only allowed creation of bitcoin from scratch is through a special transaction called Coinbase (not the exchange) inserted at the start of each block in the chain to pay the miner who inserted the block.

A transaction is taken into account instantly by the network and confirmed for the first time after approximately 10 minutes. Each new confirmation reinforces the validity of the transaction in the transaction register.

Bitcoin addresses

Each user can have any number of addresses that can be created through the wallet. Each bitcoin address has a public key and a private key pair associated with it.

An address is equal to the 160-bit (20 bytes) cryptographic hash of its public key. A bitcoin address also has a prefix identifying the version number (0 by default) and a four-byte checksum. In all, a bitcoin address occupies 25 bytes.

An address is represented in ASCII format thanks to a dedicated encoding of 58 alphanumeric characters: upper and lower case numbers and letters, with the exception of the letters and numbers l, I, o and O, which Nakamoto excluded due to their resemblance in some typefaces.

Here is, as an example, the very first bitcoin address that received bitcoins.

1A1zP1eP5QGefi2DMPTfTL5SLmv7DivfNa1o6.

To use the sum contained in an output of an existing transaction crediting a bitcoin address, the user must make use in the input of a transaction of the private key corresponding to the address by signing the transaction. The network checks the validity of this signature using the public key associated with the credited address, using asymmetric cryptography techniques. The operation is repeated for each entry of the transaction.

Wallets

Each user's wallet contains their personal data, including the address, public key and private key of each of their accounts. It can also contain user-specific information built from the blockchain. For example the list of available transaction outputs or account balances.

The wallet software provides the functions of creating accounts, consulting accounts, constructing and sending transactions. There is a choice of wallet software for all varieties of devices including smartphones. They differ in the extent of their ancillary functions and in their user interface.

The information contained in a user's wallet is critical and must be strictly protected against any intrusion. If the private key of an account is lost, the user can no longer access the transactions that fund this account, nor create new transactions from it. His bitcoins are permanently lost and will stay forever in the database without being able to change address. In 2013, a user lost 7,500 bitcoins, at the time worth $7.5 million, by accidentally throwing away the hard drive that contained his private key.

The discovery of the private key of an account by another user allows this one to steal the identity of the legitimate account holder and to spend the bitcoins which would come to be there, which is equivalent to the theft of bitcoins.

The mining process

The mining operation consists of assembling transactions into "blocks", by adding a header indicating in particular the size of the block, the number of transactions recorded, the date and time, a checksum ("hash") prohibiting any modification of the block and also serving as a unique identifier for the block, as well as the identifier of the previous block.

Miners include in the blocks they constitute a particular transaction which credits them with a certain number of bitcoins created for this purpose, and incorporates specific transaction fees. However, this remuneration will only be effective if the block is definitively accepted in the blockchain by the other nodes. It is this creation of money that explains the use of the term "mining", by analogy with the exploitation of gold mines.

A block can contain any number of transactions, typically between 1000 and 2000, but the block size cannot exceed 1 megabyte (for the Bitcoin Core system).

Within a block, transactions are stored in the form of a Merkle tree. The checksum (or fingerprint) of the block is calculated by applying twice a SHA-256 hash to the sextuplet made up of the following components.

- The software version number;
- the footprint of the header of the previous block;
- the root of the block's transaction tree (which is itself an indirect fingerprint of all the block's transactions);
- the timestamp (time elapsed since January 1, 1970, in seconds);
- the “nonce”.

The calculation of this footprint is made intentionally difficult by the requirement to be less than a certain value, which is materialized by a binary representation starting with a certain number of zeros. To this end, the fingerprint contains among its components, an arbitrary 32-bit number, called the "nonce".

Even if one knows the hashes corresponding to certain nonces, the hashing makes it impossible to determine the value of the hash for a new nonce without running the algorithm again. Therefore, we can only find the appropriate nonce for the bound requirement on the value of the fingerprint by making several tests.

For a given value of the nonce, the probability of calculating a footprint less than the difficulty is very low, so many attempts must be made before this is achieved. Between 2014 and 2016, the average number of nonces that each miner had to test between each creation of blocks increased from 1 billion to 200 billion. This calculation consists of performing the same calculation a very large number of times from different data, so it lends itself well to parallel calculation.

The difficulty is readjusted every 2016 blocks to take into account the real computing power of the network and allows on average to add a block every 10 minutes, which amounts to saying that the probable duration of calculation of a valid footprint is 10 minutes for the most powerful computer or group of computers on the network.

This system of proof of work and chaining of blocks by their footprint makes any alteration of the blockchain practically impossible (except in the case of a 51% attack). An attacker who wishes to modify a transaction in a given block would be forced to recalculate his checksum and that of all subsequent blocks. As the difficulty increases over time, as does the number of blocks after the modified transaction (its degree of confirmation), the time required to make such a modification increases very rapidly.

When a miner has built a valid block whose checksum satisfies the difficulty condition, it broadcasts it to neighboring nodes, who check its validity before reposting it in turn. The remuneration for mining work is made in bitcoin. The payout is known as the block reward. The current block reward is 6.25 bitcoins. This reward is halved for every 210,000 blocks.

The valid blocks are thus broadcast step by step to all the nodes of the network, not without having been checked beforehand, but without being able to be modified. From the nonce included in the header, it is quick and easy to check the validity of the block (a simplistic parallel can be made with a sudoku game: its resolution is difficult and requires time and human calculation but its verification is very easy once the solution is found).

The environment dilemma

Mining is an activity often criticized because of the supposed environmental imprint of its energy consumption. However, some observers weigh down the criticism by pointing out that the "classic" monetary network consumes much more energy, through millions of cash dispensers or the infrastructures necessary for the proper functioning of the classic monetary system, such as data centers. The majority of bitcoin miners use renewable energy because it is cheaper in regions of the world that favor mining (low temperature, presence of dams, geothermal energy, etc.).

Estimate of power consumption

The power consumption of Bitcoin mining is difficult to assess due to the decentralization of the activity. The figures most often cited by the press come from the "Digiconomist" site created by a Dutch financial analyst.

According to his estimate, which is based on the assumption of an economic balance between mining revenues and costs, the global electricity consumption caused by mining would be 71.1 TWh / year (1 terawatt-hour (TWh) = 1 billion kilowatt-hours (kWh)). This would totat to about 0.32% of global electricity consumption.

With only around 200,000 transactions per day in 2018, Bitcoin's electricity consumption would be around 1,000 kWh per transaction on July 1st, 2018. By comparison Visa consumed 0.19 TWh / year to manage 111 billion dollars. transactions in 2017 (around 300 million transactions per day), i.e. 0.001 7 kWh per transaction. Bitcoin would thus consume approximately 600,000 times more energy per transaction than Visa. Note, however, that mining consumption is independent of the number of transactions.

The estimates of the "Digiconomist" site are nevertheless contested and considered exaggerated. In fact, according to Marc Bevand, a computer security engineer, they overestimate the power consumption of Bitcoin miners by a factor of 1.5 to 2.8 (probably 2.2), which would reduce the total power consumption to 32.3 TWh / year, or 424 kWh per transaction (the equivalent of the consumption of a 1000 W radiator operating for almost 18 days).

These estimates are marred by uncertainties due to the assumptions they require, but it is possible to calculate a minimum power consumption of the Bitcoin network from verifiable data.

- The number of hashes per second: 37.1 × 1018 H / s on July 1st, 2018;

- the power and chopping capacity of the most efficient machine on the market (Bitmain's Antminer S9): 1323 W for 13.5 × 1012 H / s.

It is thus possible to affirm that the Bitcoin network had at least 2.8 million mining machines on July 1st, 2018 and that its electricity consumption was at least equal to 32.2 TWh / year. The number of entities securing the Bitcoin network is constantly increasing which increases the value of bitcoins.

According to a Bank of America report published in March 2021, the bitcoin network consumed 0.4% of global electricity at the end of 2020, or about as much as the Netherlands, and emits as many greenhouse gases as oil burned by American Airlines. In two years, these emissions have increased by 40 million tonnes, the equivalent of 8.3 million cars, to reach 60 million tonnes. Three quarters of the world's mining capacity is based in China; 27% of Chinese miners are in Sichuan, a province with strong low-carbon hydroelectric production, but 43% are in Xinjiang, where 80% of electricity comes from coal-fired power stations.

Why is power consumption so important?

The very high energy consumption of Bitcoin is linked to the new block mining system, which is supposed to protect the system from fraud in the absence of a central authority. Security is based on a mathematical problem the solution of which is difficult to find and the resolution of which is inherently expensive. To have a chance of adding the next block to the chain, miners must indeed invest heavily in server farms in order to have great computing power. These farms use a lot of electricity to power and cool the servers.

To be able to register a new block on the blockchain, miners must solve a mathematical problem submitted to everyone who competes, and it is the first who finds a solution that proceeds to the registration and earns a fee in bitcoins. Since the solution can only be found by trial and error, it is the miner who is able to make the maximum number of tries who has the most chance of winning. The difficulty of the problem is adjusted so that the computation time necessary for its resolution is of the order of 10 minutes.

The magnitude of the electricity consumption is linked to the intensity of the calculations and to the fact that these calculations are made simultaneously by a large number of miners. It is linked to the price of Bitcoin, because the higher it is, the more the remuneration increases and the more miners there are. This is reminiscent of Henry Ford's prediction at the start of the twentieth century: "An energy currency will replace gold and end wars".

According to Fabrice Flipo and Michel Berne, of the Institut Mines-Télécom, the generalization of crypto-currencies could lead to an energy consumption greater than eight times the electricity consumption of France, i.e. twice that of the United States, because their security and the confidence we have in them are based on a mathematical problem whose answer is difficult to find and whose resolution is in essence expensive.

The optimization of equipment and technical progress would make it possible to consume only 417 MW by 2021, which would nevertheless require nearly 5,500 kWh to produce a bitcoin, i.e. half of the annual electricity consumption of an American household.

Thus, for researcher Nicolas Houy, of the Lyon/Saint-Étienne Analysis and Economic Theory Group, "a large amount of money could very well be managed by a small amount of miners".

Groups of miners

The difficulty of mining has led miners to group together in mining pools to combine their computing resources and build new blocks more quickly. The remuneration corresponding to the constitution of each block is then divided proportionally between the members, after deduction of fees, which makes it possible to smooth their income and makes them less uncertain. In 2016, around ten of these cooperatives supplied 95% of the blocks. They are largely found in China (which accounts for most of the hash energy on the bitcoin network), but also in the Czech Republic and Georgia.

Remuneration for mining activities has led to the development of ever more specialized technologies. The most efficient hardware uses integrated circuits that outperform general-purpose processors while using less power. As of 2015, a miner not using equipment specially designed for mining had a low probability of covering his electricity and equipment costs, even by joining a mining group.

Chapter 5 - The Blockchain

The blockchain of the Bitcoin system is comparable to a public ledger recording transactions. It exists in more than 10,000 copies managed in parallel by the nodes of the network, none playing a privileged role. Some copies of the register are stored in areas safe from any cataclysm, such as in a bunker under the mountains in Switzerland.

The operator of each node in the network can decide to install a “full node” which builds and maintains a local copy of the blockchain. On the contrary, the operator can choose to be satisfied with a lightweight node which will call on the neighboring full nodes to validate the transactions using the SPV (simple payment verification) protocol.

Since these decisions are completely decentralized, it is impossible to know the number of nodes of each type. The only type permanently identified by specialized sites such as blockchain.info or bitnodes is that of “listening nodes” which accept, at the time of measurement, transactions and blocks from other nodes. Their number hovers around 10,000.

Network nodes are likely to number in the tens of thousands. For full nodes, the number of which matches the number of copies in the blockchain, estimates range from 5,000 to 30,000, located in 85 countries on all continents.

This redundancy ensures continuity of service. Each computer can become disconnected or crash without jeopardizing the proper functioning of the entire system. When it becomes operational again, the blockchain construction protocol it hosts automatically reconstructs the missing portion by resorting to neighboring nodes.

As long as they have access to the Internet, a user will always find a node in the network to accept and relay a write-in, and then there will be a large number of miners and full nodes, located all over the world, to register that write-up and make it accessible in the blockchain, where it will always remain accessible from any point in the world with Internet access, without being able to be modified.

This same redundancy, together with the "precautionary principle" under which each node of the network checks the validity of the information it receives before using it, makes it impossible to propagate fraudulent activities. Errors and frauds are still possible on a particular computer, whether caused by the operator of the site or by a hacker who manipulates this site; it is even possible that they are spread locally by contagion or by connivance. On the other hand, it is virtually impossible for such issues to spread to a significant percentage of the copies of the blockchain, let alone the entire network.

The construction of the blockchain

By receiving a new block, each computer managing a complete node executes a protocol leading either to the rejection of the block if it has already been received or if it is invalid, or to its addition to the local blockchain after a final check of all the writings it contains, or when it is put on hold.

Each block contains the identifier of the block that precedes it in its miner's blockchain and, in the most common case, this predecessor is the terminal block of the local chain, to which the new block is added after a final verification of its validity. The transactions contained in this new block are then validated by the node, in particular the one which pays in bitcoins the miner who created this block. This is transmitted to neighboring nodes and, step by step, to the entire network. In the event of failure during the verification of the validity of the block, it is kept pending, and is incorporated into a secondary branch of the blockchain.

If the node receives a new block that contains a transaction already present in the local chain, that block is rejected. It is therefore the first valid block received that each node will register in its chain of blocks. Identical blocks built by other miners in the same 10 minute cycle will be rejected, so the miners race to see their blocks added to the chain and are paid accordingly.

Due to the delay required for the blocks to propagate through the network, two blocks created in the same cycle can arrive in a different order depending on the receiving nodes, which then build different versions of the register. In this case, we say that there is a fork. Most of the time, a fork is temporary, and the blockchain construction protocol corrects it in the next cycle.

The consensus mechanism

In order for all copies of the blockchain to be identical on all nodes, even though they are built independently, this protocol incorporates a so-called "consensus" mechanism, which is a central part of the system. The rule used by Bitcoin is to retain the chain whose construction of the blocks that make it up has required the most important work. To this end, the header of each block indicates the difficulty of the work that was done to build it. The fact that the checksum of the block respects the imposed constraints constitutes the “proof of work” guaranteeing that this work has been carried out.

If, after adding a block to a secondary chain, it appears that the secondary chain required more work than the main chain, that secondary chain should become the main branch. To do this, the program goes back to where it was detached from the main branch, revalidates the blocks and the transactions they contain one by one, and adds each block at the end of the new chain being processed.

This very complex process is the real heart of the system because it is the only way to change the blockchain and its results are irreversible. It also provides functions such as the resolution of bifurcation cases and the reconstruction of the chain in the event of a computer or network shutdown.

At the end of this second phase, each of the thousands of copies of the blockchain that exist on the complete nodes was extended by a block chosen by each node from among the proposals of the miners by applying the programmed consensus rule. If all full nodes implement the same write and block validation rules, this additional block is the same for all nodes, so that all copies of the blockchain remain the same. A few thousand new transactions are thus recorded definitively and become accessible on the thousands of corresponding sites.

The role of cryptography

Cryptography is used to authenticate actors, but digital data is not encrypted: cryptography is only used to ensure the signature.

Signature keys

To be valid, each transaction must be signed, in the cryptographic sense of the term, using asymmetric cryptography techniques. To this end, each bitcoin address also constitutes the cryptographic fingerprint of a public key. Any transaction indicates as input the reference of a previous transaction justifying the availability of funds subject to the transaction and as output one or more bitcoin addresses and the amounts that must be allocated to them. A transaction always balances its inputs and outputs.

To transmit bitcoins, a user must cryptographically sign a transaction referring as input to one or more previous transactions whose output amount is sufficient to cover the transaction. The private key used to sign this transaction must match the public key that previously received bitcoins. Therefore, the user must store all his private keys in a confidential and secure manner. The corresponding file in the software, called wallet.dat, must be kept and saved by the user in a confidential manner.

Cryptography enables the authentication and non-repudiation described above, through transaction signing and one-way functions. At no time does the system ensure the confidentiality or encryption of data transmitted over the network. All transactions are therefore in the clear.

The signing of transactions is performed using elliptical curve cryptography, known as ECDSA. In this case, the curve used is secp256k1.

Transparency

Even if the software does not use any personal data of the user, anonymity is not guaranteed. In fact, the identity of a user can be determined if the IP address is traceable, or possibly as a result of a meticulous and complex statistical study of the transaction database, or when the regulations of a state or group of states take legal steps to end the anonymity of transactions on virtual currency platforms. However, it is possible to remain anonymous on the Bitcoin network with so-called "mixing" services and a good knowledge of AML, and KYC measures applied to exchange platforms.

The Bitcoin system does not encrypt any of the data it uses. Cryptography is only used to create tamper-proof signatures and implement one-way functions. Only the private key wallet is likely to be encrypted by the user, but this is optional.

Proof of work

Bitcoin uses the proof of work method, initially imagined to solve the spam problem and in particular implemented in the Hashcash system. The hash algorithms are SHA-256 and RIPEMD-160. A double hash in SHA-256 is used to obtain the hash of the blocks and therefore the proof of work, while a SHA-256 followed by a RIPEMD-160 is used to construct the bitcoin addresses.

Chapter 6 - The specific features of Bitcoin

The Bitcoin system's unit of account is bitcoin. The symbols used to represent it are BTC and XBT. Bitcoin can also be subdivided into smaller units such as millibitcoin (mXBT), microbitcoin (μXBT) or even satoshi, which represents 10 nano bitcoins (10nXBT). Microbitcoin is sometimes referred to as a bit.

The Unicode consortium agreed in November 2015 to add bitcoin among its characters, assigning it the code 20BF.

Specificities of Bitcoin

As a virtual currency, bitcoin has three particularities.

- In terms of regulation, the lack of legal status and regulatory framework means that virtual currencies do not provide any guarantee of price or liquidity. The voluntary limitation of the number of units issued without indexation carries a risk of speculation leading to high volatility.

- In terms of transparency, encryption of the identities of beneficiaries and order givers leads to total anonymity of transactions. The transactions carried out are recorded in a public register, but this traceability is limited. In fact, it does not allow to know the principal and the beneficial owner, it is neither certain nor systematic, it cannot be exploited neither technically nor legally.

- In terms of extraterritoriality, the protagonists, the servers and the legal persons who exploit them may be located in countries and territories whose cooperation may be difficult to obtain.

Exchange terminals allow bitcoin virtual currency to be exchanged for legal tender, much like an ATM can withdraw cash from a bank. To do this, these terminals can take into account identification formalities based on biometric control: taking palm prints, scanning an identity document and comparing facial features with the photo that appears on the identity card.

Another particularity of Bitcoin is the irrevocability of an illicit transaction, which makes it extremely important to be sure to send the funds to a correct address.

Proof of ownership

The user who owns bitcoins can access them through a specific address and a password also known as a private key. Since knowledge of the private key is essential for signing transactions, bitcoins cannot be spent without resorting to it. The network checks the validity of the private key using the user's public key with asymmetric cryptography techniques. On the other hand, only knowledge of the public key of an address is necessary to make a deposit. You can imagine the public key to be your bank account number, while the private key is the password to access your home banking.

Transactions and fees

Bitcoins from different transactions cannot be combined. A user receiving several payments will keep as many different amounts (called input data) in their wallet, even if their software, to make them easier to read, displays the total amount. When the user wants to spend them, their software will calculate the best set of input data to transfer to minimize the size of the output data and thus limit transaction costs.

Example: a user receives 13 payments of 1 × 2.3 XBT, 5 × 1.0 XBT, 2 × 0.7 XBT, 1 × 0.5 XBT, 1 × 0.3 XBT, 2 × 0.2 XBT and 1 × 0.1 XBT. The software will tell them that they have 10.0 XBT.

(Case 1): If they want to spend 3.0 XBT, the best set of output data will be to combine the 2.3 XBT and 0.7 XBT received previously.
(Case 2): If they want to spend 3.05 XBT, the best output data set is to bundle the 2.3 XBT with the 0.7 XBT received previously and split the transaction from 0.1 XBT into one exit transaction of 0.05 XBT, the other transaction fraction of 0.05 XBT being kept in the wallet.

As you can see, this process is quite complicated and requires a few internal transactions. The beauty of the Bitcoin network is that the end user does not need to do anything. Once the transaction has been issued, everything is done automatically.

The payment of transaction fees is theoretically optional, but the miners determine the order of processing of the transactions to be integrated into the new blocks according to the transaction fees offered by the users. The more a user accepts to pay high transaction fees, the faster their transaction will be processed. In the event of charges of the same amount, priority is given to the oldest transactions. Transactions made without transaction fees are processed after all others; in practice, these transactions start to be processed on average from 120 minutes and up to a potentially infinite time.

The most competitive transaction fees, which provide almost immediate confirmation, between 0 and 35 minutes on average, are around 80 satoshis / byte (0,000,000 80 XBT / byte). Thus, in 2016, for a median transaction size of 265 bytes, this represents an approximate cost of 21,200 satoshis (or less than $0.11) regardless of the amount of bitcoins to be transferred.

To discourage the proliferation of low-value transactions, the software applies a mandatory transaction fee of 0.0001 XBT to any transaction for an amount less than 0.01 XBT.

The larger the assemblies of input data are to carry out a transaction, the longer it takes to encode and the more the costs increase, while still remaining a very low overall amount. The algorithm of the Bitcoin software is designed to avoid as much as possible the aggregation of input data of amount less than 0.01 XBT in order to limit mandatory transaction fees.

If the amount of bitcoins to be transferred is low or if the transaction is recent, only the payment of transaction fees will allow immediate processing of the transaction. In fact, each transaction is assigned an order of priority determined as a function of its amount, its age and its size, itself determined as a function of the number of input data grouped together. Specifically, the software calculates a quotient determined by the number of bitcoins to be transferred multiplied by the age of the transaction and divided by the size of the aggregated input data. Below a certain quotient, the transaction will only be processed immediately in return for the payment of transaction fees.

If the user chooses not to pay transaction fees, the quotient will increase over time until it exceeds a threshold value which will trigger the processing of the transaction; it will thus be processed free of charge but with delay.

The higher the number of bitcoins to be transferred, the higher the quotient and the faster the user will see their transaction processed or free of charge.

For the same amount of bitcoins to be transferred, transactions involving a small number of input data are processed faster than others. Bitcoin software generally calculates the optimal fees to pay for the transaction to be processed at the time of transfer. These fees vary depending on the number of transactions to be processed at the time of the transfer, but overall they are very negligible. The user decides on their own how much transaction fees they are willing to pay.

Special cases

If a user has registered in their wallet 3 XBTs from two transactions of 1 and 2 XBT and wishes to purchase a product or service costing 2,999 XBT free of charge, the Bitcoin software will have to combine the two transactions and split the transaction of 1 XBT into one line of 0.999 XBT and one of 0.001 XBT. But in this case, the 0.001 XBT line would have an automatic charge of 0.0001 XBT applied. The user could not then make their purchase which would cost them 2 XBT + 0.999 XBT + 0.0001 XBT when they have 3 XBT and wish to keep 0.001 XBT. In such a case, it would be better for them to send 3 XBT to the seller free of charge, although some sellers want the exact purchase amount sent to them.

The reddit site reports the case of a user who won a jackpot of XBT 1,280 on a gambling site where the amount of bets was XBT 0.02. To transfer the jackpot amount, the gaming site had to aggregate 64,000 transactions amounting to XBT 0.02 in input data, which represented a 51,203 byte transaction; the amount of fees required for immediate processing was 0.026 XBT, or approximately $15, which is more than the player's bet amount, $12, or than a fee usually paid for a normal transaction- Some miners may choose to process transactions by breaking the rules of the Bitcoin protocol. In this case, they include the transaction in a new block that they will manage to mine in a longer time as their computing power is low.

The creation of bitcoins

The creation of a new block is rewarded with bitcoins created for this purpose. The amount of this reward is halved every time 210,000 transaction blocks are added to the blockchain. This process is called the "halving" and it is one of the fundamental reasons that sustain the price increase of bitcoin. Here is how it works.

From the creation of the first block (genesis block) to the 209,999th block, created on November 28, 2012, each miner was rewarded with 50 newly created bitcoins for the creation of a new valid block. From block 210,000 to block 419,999, created on July 9th, 2016, the reward was 25 bitcoins for each newly created block. From block 420,000 to block 629,999, created on May 11th, 2020, the reward was 12.5 bitcoins for each newly created block. From block 630,000 to block 839,999, the reward is 6.25 bitcoins for each newly created block.

The next halving should take place around May 2024, when the reward will decrease to 3.125 bitcoins per block.

The reward system tends towards zero as the series of 210,000 blocks follow one another, so that a maximum of 20,999,999.9769 bitcoins will be created, probably around the year 2140. The gradual decrease in the amount of new bitcoins rewarding the creation of new blocks will be offset by the development of transaction fees.

In other words, the inventor of the Bitcoin system tried to define a monetary policy whereby the number of bitcoins cannot exceed 21 million units in total, with the rate of creation of new units tending towards zero. Such a monetary system is described as deflationary. As you might know, the Dollar-based system is inflationary, as more units are printed to sustain the growth of the economy.

Confidentiality

The Bitcoin system indicates on the public ledger the amount of bitcoins associated with each address. All transactions recorded on the blockchain are also public. The identity of the owners of bitcoin addresses is not public but can be determined, for example through exchange platforms that record the identity of their users.

Exchange platforms generally pool their users' holdings on a single address and reallocate a bitcoin credit line to each of their users through their trading software. Users can thus exchange their bitcoins for other cryptocurrencies or for currencies. The platform secures its deposits by distributing them over several addresses or by storing them to prevent any theft. When a user transfers the deposits from the platform to another address, the platform debits the credit line and transfers the amount to be exchanged from one of his addresses to the address indicated by the user.

Researchers at Stanford University and Concordia University have shown that, to prevent hacking, bitcoin exchange platforms can prove their creditworthiness without revealing their addresses using zero-knowledge protocols.

It is also possible to keep bitcoins in "cold storage" on a digital medium disconnected from the network, which has the effect of protecting them against theft. Between 2017 and 2018, a French start-up sold more than 1.5 million of these bitcoin safes in 165 countries Nowadays, Ledger and Trezor are the two main companies that sell hard wallets.

Researchers have argued that in the absence of specific protection measures, payments made using the Bitcoin protocol are no more private than payments by bank card.

Stock exchanges and financial instruments

Bitcoin, as a virtual currency, is quite unclassifiable. Thus, some asset management companies consider that virtual currency can neither be considered as a good investment, nor be compared to gold, due to the lack of price history.

For the ex-president of the SEC, Jay Clayton, the "Initial Coin Offerings" are less protected than the traditional securities, allowing more manipulation of markets and scams. For him, as for other investments, extreme caution as well as awareness of the risk of losing everything is required.

No ICOs have been registered with the US federal financial markets regulator and supervisor (known as the SEC), and the listing and trading of exchange traded products that hold cryptocurrency has not been approved by the SEC up to this point.

Market platforms

Fiduciary currencies (USD, EUR, CNY, etc.) or crypto-currencies (ETH, LTC, etc.) can be exchanged for bitcoins through various exchanges or specialized trading platforms active on the internet, by carrying out transactions transfers by bank transfer. Brokerage fees are generally very low and users must provide proof of their identity to access these platforms. As you might think, in this way the anonymity of Bitcoin disappears.

Escrow platforms connect buyers and sellers to exchange bitcoins for cash, money orders, or bank transfers.
One-way points of sale make it possible to pay in bitcoins, subject to the payment of a fee, by debiting the corresponding amount in dollars on bank cards or prepaid cards.

Finally, there are vending machines which charge a generally higher commission.

Since November 2016, the Swiss Federal Railways have been offering, in conjunction with the company SweePay, the purchase of bitcoins from their train ticket machines, thus creating the largest bitcoin distribution network in the world.

Chapter 7 - Satoshi Nakamoto

As we have seen, the creation of the Bitcoin network is still a mystery. In this chapter we try to gather all the information there is regarding the identity of Satoshi Nakamoto. Please, keep in mind that his identity has never been revealed and that we can only make assumptions on who he actually is.

Satoshi Nakamoto is the pseudonym of the inventor of the cryptocurrency Bitcoin.

In November 2008, Satoshi Nakamoto published the Bitcoin protocol on The Cryptography Mailing list on the metzdowd.com website. In 2009 he distributed the first version of the client software and later contributed to the project anonymously together with other developers, to finally withdraw from the Bitcoin community in 2010. The last contact from Satoshi Nakamoto was in 2011, when he claimed to have moved on to other projects and left Bitcoin in good hands with Gavin Andresen.

The theories about Satoshi Nakamoto's true identity are numerous. Nobody knows if it is a "he", a "she" or if it is more than one person. In Japanese "satoshi" means "clear, quick and wise thought". "Naka" can mean "medium", "inside" or "relationship". "Moto" can mean "origin" or "foundation". But it is not certain whether these meanings are useful to trace back to the person or group of people who invented the Bitcoin system.

It was originally thought to be Michael Clear, a graduate in cryptography from Trinity College but he denied. Others suspected Vili Lehdonvirta, a former Finnish game developer (but also a sociologist and economist), but he too has denied any connection with Satoshi.

Adam Penenberg, a professor at New York University, claims that behind the mysterious character there are three people: Neal King, Vladimir Oksman, Charles Bry. Penenberg's thesis is based on a Google search of some particular phrases of the bitcoin protocol that lead back to a patent request for updating and distributing cryptographic keys. The patent was applied for by King, Oksman and Bry, who denied having anything to do with bitcoin.

Nick Szabo, a computer scientist and cryptographer, has long been suspected of being Satoshi along with collaborator Laszlo Hanyecz. Both have always firmly denied, but in the next pages we are going to tell you more about Szabo, as he is the one we believe to be Satoshi.

Others think it is Martii Malmi, a Finnish developer, who dealt with Bitcoin from the very beginning by also creating the user interface of the system. There are also rumors about the creator of MtGox, Jed McCaleb, an American lover of Japanese culture and resident in Japan. Other theories instead lead to Donal O'Mahony and Michael Peirce, who wrote a paper on digital payments in e-commerce platforms.

In 2017, after a tip from a SpaceX employee, the idea appeared on the web that Elon Musk was hiding behind the pseudonym, a theory later denied by the entrepreneur himself on his Twitter account.

Craig Steven Wright

In December 2015, according to two investigative articles published by Wired and Gizmodo, Craig Steven Wright, an Australian entrepreneur, would be the creator of Bitcoin. Within hours, searches were carried out in Wright's home and office by the Australian Federal Police, however unrelated to the incident.

On May 2nd, 2016, Craig Steven Wright publicly claimed to be Satoshi Nakamoto. Wright revealed his identity to the BBC, The Economist and GQ. In order to prove his claim, he signed a message with the private encryption key associated with the first Bitcoin transaction. However, the validation of this signature is disputed and even if its validity were demonstrated, many cryptographic experts do not consider it a definitive proof, as it refers to the second block and not to the first created.

On May 4th, 2016, Wright promised to publish further evidence to prove his identity. However, the next day, he deleted all posts on his blog and published a note titled "I'm sorry" in which he declared that he was ready to publish more evidence but did not have the courage to do so. He ended the note with a "goodbye". In the same year Wright filed a copyright request for the Bitcoin white paper, originally written by Satoshi Nakamoto. However, the copyright request was denied due to insufficient proof of ownership.

Nick Szabo

We admit it: our opinion is that Nick Szabo is Satoshi Nakamoto. We have no actual proof of his identity, but after having researched this subject quite extensively this is our opinion.

Nick Szabo is a computer scientist, lawyer, and cryptographer known for his research on digital contracts and digital currency. He graduated from the University of Washington in 1989 with a degree in computer science.The expression and concept of "smart contracts" were developed by Szabo with the aim of bringing what he calls "highly evolved" practices of contract law, from the conception to the application of the protocols of contract between strangers on the Internet. Smart contracts are a major feature of cryptocurrencies and the programming language E.

Szabo worked for David Chaum, the inventor of electronic money "E-Cash" as a consultant in the mid-90s. In 1998, Szabo designed a decentralized digital currency mechanism which he called "Bit gold". Bit gold, not having received enough support, was never implemented, but was referred to as a direct precursor to the Bitcoin architecture.

In the principle of Bit gold, participants devote the power of their computers to solving cryptographic puzzles. The solved puzzles are sent to a public registry insensitive to the problem of the Byzantine generals, and assigned to the public key of the participant who solved the puzzle. Each solution is then integrated into the input data of the next challenge, creating an increasingly long chain. Until the majority of participants agree to a solution for the current riddle, the work of solving the next riddle cannot begin. It is a proof-of-work-type consensus model. This also makes it possible to manage the issuance of new Bit gold tokens as well as a means of checking their timestamp.

The main problem with transactions in digital form is the so-called

double-spending problem. Once the data has been created, reproducing it is a simple matter of copying and pasting. Most digital currencies solve the problem by ceding some control to a central authority that keeps track of the balance of each account. This was considered unacceptable by Szabo. In an interview he stated the following. “I sought to imitate as closely as possible in cyberspace the security and trust characteristics of gold, and the main one is that it does not depend on any central authority”.

In 2008, a mysterious figure writing under the pseudonym Satoshi Nakamoto published a proposal for Bitcoin. As you know Nakamoto's true identity has since remained a secret, leading to speculation about a long list of people suspected of being Nakamoto. Although Szabo has repeatedly denied it, some people (including us) have speculated that he was Nakamoto.

Research by financial author Dominic Frisby provides circumstantial evidence of this, but, as he admits, no formal evidence that Satoshi is indeed Szabo. In a July 2014 email from Frisby, Szabo said, “Thanks for letting me know this. I'm afraid you are wrong in exposing me as Satoshi, but I'm used to this".

Nathaniel Popper wrote in the New York Times that the most convincing evidence regarding the creation of Bitcoin pointed to an American man of Hungarian descent by the name of Nick Szabo. In

2008, prior to the publication of Bitcoin, Szabo wrote a comment on his blog about the intention to create a working version of his hypothetical currency. This blog post is exactly what makes us think he is the actual inventor of this amazing monetary network.

Chapter 8 - The Byzantine Generals Problem

In the previous chapters, we have mentioned the Byzantine generals problem a few times. In the next few pages we are going to dive deeper into this subject and understand why Bitcoin offers an amazing solution to this issue.

The problem of the Byzantine generals is a computer problem on how to reach consensus in situations where errors are possible. In particular, in distributed computer systems there may be imperfect information for the failure of a component, such as a server, and it can appear inconsistent, non-functional and functioning for fault detection systems, presenting different symptoms to different observers.

The problem

The problem of the Byzantine generals refers to a problem of agreement (described by Leslie Lamport, Robert Shostak and Marshall Pease in their 1982 article "The problem of the Byzantine generals") in which a group of generals commands part of the Byzantine army. Surrounded by a city, these generals want to formulate a plan to attack it. In its simplest form, generals should only decide whether to attack or retreat, and some generals prefer to attack, while others prefer to retreat. The important thing is that each general accepts a common decision, as a solitary attack by some generals would result in a defeat and would be worse than a coordinated attack or a coordinated withdrawal.

The problem is complicated by the presence of traitorous generals who not only vote for a suboptimal strategy, but can do so selectively. For example, if nine generals vote, four of whom support the attack while the other four are in favor of the withdrawal, the ninth general can send a vote of withdrawal to those generals in favor of the withdrawal and an attack vote to the others. Those who have received a vote of withdrawal from the ninth general will withdraw, while the rest will attack. The problem is further complicated by the fact that the generals are physically separated and must send their votes through messengers who may not report the votes or falsify them.

Byzantine fault tolerance can be achieved if loyal (non-defective) generals find majority agreement on their strategy. Note that there may be a default vote value for lost messages. For example, missing messages can be assigned the value <null>. In addition, if the agreement provides that the <null> votes are the majority, it is possible to use a pre-established strategy (for example, withdrawal).

The typical mapping of this story into computer systems is that computers are the generals and their connections to the digital communications system are the messengers. Although the problem is formulated in the analogy as a decision-making and security problem, in electronics it cannot be solved simply with cryptographic digital signatures, since errors such as incorrect voltages can be propagated through the encryption process. Therefore, a component may appear to be functional for one component and defective for another component, which prevents a consensus on whether the component is defective or not.

Examples of Byzantine errors

In a similar problem, bee swarms are used as an example. They have to find a new home, and the bees have to reach a consensus on which of the candidate homes they can reach. And then everyone has to fly there, with their queen. The bee approach works reliably, but when researchers find two houses, equally attractive by all bee criteria, a catastrophe occurs, the swarm breaks up and all the bees die.

First solutions

In 1982 Lamport, Shostak and Pease described several solutions. They began by pointing out that the problem of generals can be reduced to solve a "commander and lieutenant" problem in which loyal lieutenants must act in group and that their action must correspond to that the commander has ordered in case the commander is loyal.

One solution considers scenarios in which messages can be falsified, but which will be tolerant of Byzantine flaws as long as the number of traitorous generals does not equal or exceed one third of the generals. The inability to deal with a third or more of the traitors ultimately boils down to proving that the problem of one commander and two lieutenants cannot be solved if the commander is a traitor. To see this, suppose we have a treacherous commander A and two lieutenants, B and C. When A tells B to attack and C to retreat, and B and C exchange messages, relaying the message from A, neither B nor C can find out who the traitor is, since it is not necessarily A. In fact, another lieutenant could have falsified the message presumably from A.

It can be shown that if "n" is the number of generals in total, and "t" is the number of traitors in that n, there are solutions to the problem only when $n>3t$ and the communication is synchronous.

A second solution requires unforced message signatures. For critical security systems, digital signatures (in modern computer systems, this can be achieved in practice using public key cryptography) can provide tolerance to Byzantine flaws in the presence of an arbitrary number of traitorous generals.

There is also a variation of the first two solutions that allow for behavior tolerant to Byzantine errors in some situations where not all generals can communicate directly with each other.

Around 1980, several system architectures that implemented Byzantine fault tolerance were designed. These include: Draper's FTMP, Honeywell13's 12 MMFC, and SRI.14's SIFT

Fault tolerance

In 1999, Miguel Castro and Barbara Liskov introduced the "BFT (Byzantine Fault Tolerance) algorithm. In a nutshell, Byzantine fault tolerance (BFT) is the property of a system that can resist the class of failures derived from the Byzantine generals Problem. This means that a BFT system is able to continue operating even if some nodes fail or act dishonestly.

There is more than one solution to the Byzantine generals problem and, consequently, more than one way to build a BFT system. Likewise, there are various different approaches for a blockchain that intends to achieve Byzantine fault tolerance. This brings us to so-called consensus algorithms.

Bitcoin and the BFT algorithm

An example of BFT in use is bitcoin, a peer-to-peer digital currency system. The bitcoin network works in parallel to generate a Hashcash-style work test chain. The proof-of-work chain is the key to overcoming Byzantine failures and obtaining a coherent global view of the state of the system.

We can define a consensus algorithm as the mechanism by which a blockchain network achieves consensus. The most common implementations are proof of work (PoW) and proof of stake (PoS). Let's take the case of Bitcoin as an example.

While the Bitcoin protocol establishes the primary rules of the system, the PoW consensus algorithm is what defines the way these rules are followed to reach consensus (for example, when verifying and validating transactions). Even though the concept of proof of work is older than cryptocurrencies, Satoshi Nakamoto developed a modified version by creating an algorithm that allowed the creation of Bitcoin as a BFT system.

It should be remembered that the PoW algorithm is not 100% Byzantine fault tolerant, but thanks to the expensive mining process and the underlying cryptographic techniques, PoW has proved to be one of the safest and most reliable implementations for blockchain networks. In this sense, the Proof of Work consensus algorithm, designed by Satoshi Nakamoto, is considered by many to be one of the most ingenious solutions to the Byzantine Generals Problem.

As we have seen, the Byzantine Generals Problem is an interesting dilemma that eventually gave rise to BFT systems, which are widely applied in different scenarios. In addition to the blockchain sector, some use cases for BFT systems include aviation, space industry and nuclear energy.

In the context of cryptocurrencies, having efficient network communication along with a valid consensus mechanism is vital for any blockchain ecosystem. Securing these systems is a constant effort, and existing consensus algorithms have not yet managed to overcome certain limitations (such as scalability). Despite this, PoW and PoS are very interesting approaches as BFT systems, and the potential applications are certainly inspiring widespread innovation.

Conclusion

Congratulations on making it to the end of this book, we hope you found some useful insights to take your cryptocurrency trading skills to the next level. As you should know by now, the world of Bitcoin is extremely complicated and there is a new "opportunity" every way you look. However, our experience tells us that only by taking things seriously and having a proper plan you can develop your investing skills to the point that you can actually accumulate wealth.

Our final advice is to stay away from the shining objects that the world of cryptocurrencies offers you every day. Simply dollar cost average into Bitcoin and study the world of cryptocurrencies in depth. After you have sufficient knowledge on what you are talking about, you can go ahead and invest into other cryptocurrencies. Analyze your results, improve your money management skills and become the master of your emotions.

As you can see, there are no shortcuts you can take. Easy money does not exist. What exists is the possibility to start from zero and work your way up to become a professional Bitcoin investor. The journey might be difficult, but it is certainly worth it.

To your success!

BITCOIN DIGITAL CRYPTOCURRENCY - BITCOIN DIGITAL CRYPTOCURRENCY - BITCOIN DIGITAL CRYPTOCURRENCY -

CPSIA information can be obtained
at www.ICGtesting.com
Printed in the USA
BVHW091053140521
607266BV00004BA/923

9 781802 661972